Automated Realities Shaping Tomorrow_s Work

Automated Realities Shaping Tomorrow_s Work

Alina Hazel

Noble Publishing

CONTENTS

1

INDEX

Chapter 4: Adapting to Workplace Transformation
4.1 Remote Work: Automation's Catalyst

4.2 Redefining Job Structures in Automated Industries

4.3 Upskilling and Reskilling Initiatives in the Automated Era

4.4 Balancing Flexibility and Security in Automated Work Environments

Chapter 5: Upskilling Initiatives
5.1 The Need for Upskilling and Reskilling

5.2 Innovative Approaches to Workforce Training

5.3 Technology-Enabled Learning Platforms

5.4 Corporate Responsibility in Employee Development

Chapter 6: Socioeconomic Impact
6.1 Addressing Socioeconomic Disparities

6.2 Policy Frameworks for a Balanced Automated Workforce

6.3 The Role of Governments in Managing Transition

6.4 Socioeconomic Implications of Remote Work

Chapter 7: The Future Work Ecosystem
7.1 Embracing the Automated Future

7.2 Building Sustainable and Adaptable Careers

7.3 Prospects for Future Jobs in Automated Industries

7.4 The Continuous Evolution of Work in Automated Realities

Introduction

In the steadily developing scene of the contemporary world, the convergence of innovation and human undertaking has led to a change in outlook in the manner in which we see and draw in with work. As we stand at the limit of another period, set apart by uncommon progressions in robotization and man-made brainpower, the actual texture of our expert presence is going through a significant change. This change, portrayed by the combination of robotized truths, is molding the shapes of the upcoming work in manners that are both sensational and testing.

The quick speed of mechanical advancement has introduced a time where robotization is not generally bound to the domain of sci-fi yet has turned into a basic piece of our regular routines. From savvy homes that expect our requirements to self-driving vehicles exploring the roads, the ringlets of computerization have saturated each part of our reality. In this specific situation, the working environment remains as a cauldron where the mixture of human capacities and mechanical ability is manufacturing new wildernesses.

At the core of this change lies man-made reasoning (simulated intelligence), a field that has seen uncommon development and refinement lately. AI calculations, brain organizations, and normal language handling have engaged machines to perform routine errands as well as to learn, adjust, and pursue choices in manners that were once remembered to be the selective area of human comprehension. As man-made intelligence keeps on advancing, its effect on the universe of work is turning out to be progressively articulated.

The ascent of computerized real factors in the work environment is reshaping conventional thoughts of business, efficiency, and occupation jobs. Assignments that were once performed by human specialists are currently being computerized, prompting expanded effectiveness and accuracy. Normal and dull positions are being moved to machines, opening up human resources to zero in on assignments that require imagination, decisive reasoning, and the ability to appreciate anyone at their core. This change in the division of work is testing laid out ideal models and rethinking the actual substance of being utilized in the 21st 100 years.

While computerization carries with it the commitment of expanded proficiency and efficiency, it additionally raises worries about the relocation of human specialists. The anxiety toward employment cutback because of robotization has turned into a predominant topic openly talk, with inquiries concerning the eventual fate of work and the job of people in an undeniably computerized world becoming the overwhelming focus. As machines take on additional obligations, the test lies in guaranteeing that the advantages of robotization are impartially disseminated, and the potential for social and monetary disparity is relieved.

One of the remarkable fields where robotized truths are applying a groundbreaking impact is in the domain of mechanical technology. The approach of refined mechanical frameworks fit for perplexing errands has extended the extent of mechanization past routine office work. Businesses like assembling, medical services, and strategies are seeing the reconciliation of automated innovations that increase human capacities and reclassify the idea of work. Cooperative robots, or cobots, are working close by people, improving efficiency and security in different settings.

In addition, the expansion of robotized frameworks isn't restricted to actual errands alone; it reaches out into the advanced domain too. The ascent of mechanical cycle mechanization (RPA) has empowered associations to computerize dull and administer based advanced errands, going from information passage to complex dynamic cycles. As calculations become more proficient at taking care of mental undertakings, the forms of expert scenes are moving, inciting associations to reevaluate their labor force organization and ability prerequisites.

The effect of computerized real factors reaches out past the prompt circle of work to include more extensive financial contemplations. The coming of computerization can possibly reshape the elements of pay conveyance and reclassify the idea of work itself. As machines take on routine errands, the accentuation on exceptionally human credits like inventiveness, the capacity to understand anyone on a deeper level, and relational abilities turns out to be more articulated. This change in center requires a reconsideration of instructive and preparing ideal models to furnish the labor force with the abilities expected to flourish in a robotized climate.

In the midst of the extraordinary floods of computerization, the idea of remote work has acquired exceptional noticeable quality. The combination of advanced innovations, combined with the abilities of computerized frameworks, has worked with the decentralization of work, empowering people to team up and contribute from assorted geological areas. The conventional thought of the workplace as an actual space is going through a redefinition, with virtual coordinated effort stages and remote work becoming necessary parts of the contemporary expert scene.

As associations adjust to the changing elements of work, the job of authority in exploring the robotized future becomes pivotal. Pioneers are entrusted with bridling the capability of robotized advances as well as with encouraging a work culture that focuses on versatility, constant learning, and development. The capacity to figure out some kind of harmony between utilizing robotization for productivity and safeguarding the human-driven parts of work is an authority challenge that characterizes progress in the mechanized period.

The moral components of mechanization likewise come to the front as machines become progressively entwined with our expert lives. Inquiries concerning information security, algorithmic predisposition, and the social ramifications of mechanized dynamic cycles highlight the significance of moral contemplations in the plan and organization of robotized frameworks.

As mechanized real factors shape the forms of the upcoming work, moral structures should develop to guarantee that innovation fills in as a power for good, advancing inclusivity and decency.

The extraordinary effect of robotized truths isn't restricted to the corporate area alone; it stretches out to the public area, where legislatures are wrestling with the ramifications of robotization on administration and public administrations. From artificial intelligence controlled chatbots helping residents to prescient examination illuminating approach choices, the combination of robotized frameworks in policy implementation is adjusting the manner in which states connect with their constituents. Be that as it may, this mix additionally raises worries about responsibility, straightforwardness, and the potential for unseen side-effects in dynamic cycles.

In the domain of medical services, mechanized advances are changing diagnostics, therapy, and patient consideration. From mechanical helped medical procedures to simulated intelligence driven symptomatic apparatuses, the marriage of innovation and medical care is opening new outskirts in clinical advancement. The combination of robotized frameworks in medical services, in any case, prompts moral contemplations with respect to patient protection, the unwavering quality of calculations, and the potential for innovation to compound existing wellbeing abberations.

The forms of the upcoming work are additionally molded by the advancing idea of abilities and capabilities expected in the robotized period. The customary accentuation on specialized abilities is supplemented by a developing acknowledgment of the significance of delicate abilities like versatility, flexibility, and the capacity to understand people on a deeper level. The capacity to team up with robotized frameworks and influence innovation for critical thinking turns into a vital differentiator in a labor force that is exploring the intricacies of a mechanized reality.

All in all, the coming of robotized truths is introducing another period in the realm of work, described by the coordination of innovation into each aspect of expert life. The groundbreaking effect of computerization stretches out past the limits of individual work jobs to reshape enterprises, economies, and cultural designs. As we explore this time of extraordinary change, the test lies in saddling the capability of computerized advances while tending to the moral, financial, and social ramifications that go with this change in outlook. The upcoming work isn't simply a continuation of the present undertakings however a unique exchange between human resourcefulness and mechanical development, where the genuine capability of computerized truths is acknowledged in the help of a superior, more comprehensive future.

Chapter 1

The Evolution of Automation

Robotization, an idea that has gone through a groundbreaking excursion all through mankind's set of experiences, remains as a demonstration of our determined quest for effectiveness and mechanical progression. From the simple instruments of old developments to the intricate calculations overseeing present day ventures, the advancement of mechanization is an embroidery woven with advancement, challenges, and cultural ramifications.

The foundations of computerization can be followed back to ancient times when early people designed basic apparatuses to ease the weights of physical work. These instruments, created from stone, bone, and wood, denoted the most important moves towards computerizing tedious errands, liberating human hands for additional complicated undertakings. The slow movement from fundamental instruments to additional modern mechanical gadgets unfurled over hundreds of years, driven by a firmly established human craving to vanquish time and improve efficiency.

The Modern Unrest of the eighteenth and nineteenth hundreds of years denoted a urgent crossroads throughout the entire existence of mechanization. The coming of steam power and the motorization of material creation introduced a time where machines could perform undertakings recently held for talented craftsmans. The sequential construction system, an outlook changing development presented by Henry Passage in the mid twentieth 100 years, embodied the effectiveness acquires feasible through mechanization. By separating complex cycles into a progression of redundant errands, Passage's sequential construction system reformed assembling, laying the foundation for large scale manufacturing and changing the monetary scene.

As the twentieth century unfurled, the reconciliation of gadgets and PCs into modern cycles proclaimed another time of robotization. Early modernized frameworks, with their restricted abilities, were regardless instrumental in overseeing complex undertakings, offering phenomenal accuracy and control. The ascent of programmable rationale regulators (PLCs) in assembling plants additionally sped up the computerization pattern, empowering the ongoing control of apparatus and cycles. Businesses going from car assembling to substance creation saw a flood in productivity, with robotization becoming inseparable from progress.

The 21st century saw the combination of mechanization with computerized reasoning (computer based intelligence), opening new outskirts in mechanical abilities. AI calculations, equipped for breaking down tremendous datasets and adjusting to evolving conditions, engaged frameworks to settle on choices without express programming. The cooperative energy among computerization and artificial intelligence led to independent frameworks, from self-driving vehicles exploring perplexing metropolitan scenes to mechanical arms executing fragile surgeries. The time of Industry 4.0 arose, portrayed by the combination of digital actual frameworks, the Web of Things (IoT), and distributed computing.

In the domain of buyer innovation, brilliant homes turned into an unmistakable sign of mechanization's venture into regular day to day existence. Mechanized indoor regulators, lighting frameworks, and voice-enacted associates changed homes into clever environments, where machines expected and answered human requirements. The consistent mix of mechanization into everyday schedules brought up issues about protection, security, and the moral ramifications of giving up control to astute machines.

While mechanization guaranteed unmatched proficiency and accommodation, its boundless reception additionally started worries about work relocation. The apprehension about machines supplanting human work has went with each period of mechanization, from the Modern Upheaval to the current day. As standard errands became computerized, the interest for new abilities and the development of occupation jobs became basic. The requirement for a labor force capable in making due, planning, and keeping up with robotized frameworks made a change in perspective in training and expertise improvement.

The effect of robotization on business elements is a multi-layered issue. While specific positions confronted out of date quality, new open doors arose in enterprises driven by mechanical development. The ascent of the gig economy and the interest for abilities in fields like information science, man-made brainpower, and online protection mirrored the developing idea of work in the period of mechanization. Policymakers and teachers wrestled with the test of furnishing people with the abilities important to flourish in an undeniably mechanized world.

Moral contemplations encompassing mechanization reached out past business concerns. The turn of events and arrangement of independent frameworks brought up issues about responsibility, straightforwardness, and the likely results of machine direction. The moral elements of man-made intelligence, especially in delicate spaces like medical services and law enforcement, provoked a reassessment of administrative structures and the foundation of moral rules for man-made intelligence improvement.

As robotization kept on rethinking businesses and reshape cultural designs, the connection among people and machines advanced. The idea of human-machine joint effort acquired conspicuousness, stressing the increase of human abilities through innovation. In clinical fields, automated helped medical procedures exhibited the collaboration between human skill and machine accuracy. The possibility of a future where people and robots worked pair, each utilizing their interesting assets, tested customary thoughts of rivalry among man and machine.

The development of computerization rose above the limits of industry and entered the domain of metropolitan preparation and transportation. Savvy urban areas, outfitted with interconnected sensors and insightful framework, intended to improve asset use and upgrade the personal satisfaction for occupants. Mechanized transportation frameworks, including self-driving vehicles and hyperloop advancements, vowed to reform the manner in which individuals and products moved, introducing the two potential open doors and difficulties for metropolitan turn of events.

The tenacious speed of mechanical progression delivered additional opportunities and difficulties. Quantum registering, with its capability to dramatically increment handling power, indicated a future where complex issues right now past the compass of traditional PCs could be tackled. In any case, the appearance of quantum processing additionally raised worries about the security suggestions for existing cryptographic frameworks and the requirement for novel ways to deal with shield delicate data.

The democratization of mechanization devices and advancements added to an expanding society of development and business. New companies and private ventures utilized distributed computing, open-source stages, and available mechanization answers for disturb customary enterprises and make novel plans of action.

The readiness managed via mechanization engaged deft undertakings to adjust to quickly changing business sector elements, provoking laid out players to embrace development or face out of date quality.

In the domain of room investigation, mechanization assumed a vital part in expanding the scope of human investigation. Automated rocket and meanderers, furnished with cutting edge mechanization frameworks, wandered into the universe, giving significant bits of knowledge into the secrets of the universe. The possibility of independent space investigation, including the sending of mechanical missions to far off planets and space rocks, highlighted the job of robotization in pushing the limits of human information and revelation.

The development of mechanization was not without its difficulties. Network protection dangers posed a potential threat as interconnected frameworks became helpless against malevolent entertainers looking to take advantage of weaknesses. The rising dependence on robotization in basic framework, from power networks to medical services frameworks, required strong network protection measures to shield against likely disturbances and assaults.

Ecological manageability arose as a squeezing thought in the turn of events and organization of robotized advances. The energy utilization related with enormous scope computerization and server farms brought up issues about the carbon impression of innovative advancement. Developments in green advancements, combined with a developing consciousness of the ecological effect of robotization, provoked a shift towards reasonable practices in the plan and activity of computerized frameworks.

The administrative scene battled to stay up with the fast development of computerization. As independent vehicles took to the streets and simulated intelligence fueled frameworks pursued choices with sweeping outcomes, the requirement for extensive guidelines became apparent. Policymakers wrestled with characterizing legitimate systems that tended to the moral, security, and responsibility aspects of robotization, looking for a sensitive harmony between cultivating development and relieving gambles.

The cultural ramifications of robotization reached out past the monetary and innovative spaces. The appearance of social robots, intended to connect and help people in different limits, brought up issues about the idea of human connections and the moral limits of human-robot cooperations. The coordination of robotization into instruction, with the utilization of man-made intelligence fueled coaching frameworks and customized learning stages, reshaped conventional academic methodologies, introducing the two open doors and difficulties for the fate of learning.

The convergence of robotization with medical care displayed the potential for extraordinary effect. From mechanical medical procedure to computer based intelligence helped diagnostics, mechanization vowed to upgrade clinical results and work on understanding consideration.

Nonetheless, the moral contemplations encompassing the utilization of individual wellbeing information, the potential for predisposition in calculations, and inquiries of patient independence provoked a nuanced investigation of the job of computerization in the medical care scene.

As the direction of mechanization unfurled, the story stretched out past the bounds of Earth. The investigation and possible colonization of different planets delivered dreams of mechanized frameworks building environments, separating assets, and supporting human.

1.1 The Fourth Industrial Revolution

The expression "Fourth Modern Upset" (4IR) exemplifies an extraordinary period set apart by the intermingling of computerized innovations, mechanization, and the exceptional coordination of the physical, advanced, and organic circles. This epochal shift addresses a paradigmatic takeoff from the modern upsets that went before it, every one of which achieved significant changes in the public eye, economy, and innovation.

The Primary Modern Transformation, portrayed by the motorization of creation through the appearance of steam power and automated material creation, established the groundwork for industrialization in the late eighteenth 100 years. The Second Modern Upset, driven by power, the message, and the sequential construction system, unfurled in the late nineteenth and mid twentieth hundreds of years, encouraging large scale manufacturing and the ascent of modern private enterprise. The Third Modern Upset, frequently alluded to as the Advanced Unrest, arose during the twentieth hundred years with the approach of PCs, semiconductors, and the web, in a general sense modifying correspondence, business, and data scattering.

The Fourth Modern Upset, in any case, separates itself by the velocity and significance of its effect on practically every aspect of human existence. Fundamental to this upheaval is the combination of advancements that obscure the lines between the physical, computerized, and natural spaces. At the core of this union are groundbreaking innovations like computerized reasoning (simulated intelligence), the Web of Things (IoT), advanced mechanics, 3D printing, quantum processing, and biotechnology. These advances, separately strong, gain outstanding strength when incorporated into far reaching frameworks.

The unavoidable impact of the Fourth Modern Upset is most clear in the domain of computerization. The reconciliation of cutting edge mechanical technology, AI, and artificial intelligence into assembling processes has prompted the production of savvy plants. These manufacturing plants are described by interconnected machines and frameworks that can convey, examine information continuously, and adjust to evolving conditions. The outcome isn't simply expanded proficiency yet a crucial change in the idea of creation, with customization and adaptability becoming vital parts of assembling.

The Fourth Modern Transformation stretches out past the limits of industry, pervading different parts of day to day existence. The Web of Things, an organization of interconnected gadgets implanted with sensors and programming, works with the consistent trade of information. Shrewd homes, furnished with IoT gadgets, take into consideration the remote observing and control of different machines, lighting, and security frameworks. Wearable gadgets, one more appearance of IoT, track wellbeing measurements and empower people to come to informed conclusions about their prosperity.

The effect of the Fourth Modern Unrest on the labor force is significant and diverse. Mechanization, driven by mechanical technology and computer based intelligence, can possibly smooth out routine undertakings, upgrading efficiency and productivity. Be that as it may, this productivity accompanies difficulties, especially the uprooting of specific work classifications. As machines take over monotonous undertakings, there is a developing accentuation on the requirement for a labor force outfitted with abilities that supplement computerization - inventiveness, decisive reasoning, critical thinking, and versatility. The development of work in the 4IR requires a reexamination of schooling and preparing frameworks to get ready people for the requests of an undeniably robotized scene.

The Fourth Modern Upset likewise proclaims another period of availability. The expansion of rapid web, combined with the ascent of portable innovations, has made a worldwide interconnected society. Virtual entertainment stages, conceived out of the computerized transformation, work with moment correspondence and data sharing on a worldwide scale. This interconnectedness has suggestions for city commitment, social trade, and the scattering of data, molding a dynamic and interconnected worldwide local area.

In the field of medical services, the Fourth Modern Upset delivers advancements that guarantee to change diagnostics and therapy. The combination of computer based intelligence into clinical imaging considers more precise and productive determination. Wearable wellbeing gadgets, engaged by IoT, give ongoing checking of patients, empowering proactive medical care intercessions. Progresses in biotechnology, including quality altering advances like CRISPR, open roads for customized medication and the treatment of hereditary issues.

The extraordinary capability of the Fourth Modern Upheaval is maybe most apparent in the domain of man-made brainpower. AI calculations, a subset of man-made intelligence, empower frameworks to gain from information and further develop execution over the long haul without unequivocal programming. This capacity has applications across assorted fields, from regular language handling and picture acknowledgment to prescient examination and independent frameworks. The advancement of simulated intelligence brings up issues about morals, responsibility, and the cultural effect of machines settling on choices that were once the domain of human judgment.

The Fourth Modern Upset isn't without its difficulties and concerns. The fast speed of mechanical change overwhelms the capacity of administrative systems to keep up, making holes in administration and responsibility. Security concerns, especially in the time of omnipresent network and information driven navigation, brief a reexamination of moral guidelines and the insurance of individual freedoms. The potential for work relocation because of computerization requires insightful thought of social and monetary strategies to guarantee a fair and comprehensive progress to the new financial scene.

Another basic thought is the ecological effect of the innovations driving the Fourth Modern Upset. The energy prerequisites of server farms, fabricating processes, and the removal of electronic waste bring up issues about the manageability of the mechanical advancement. Developments in green advancements, combined with a developing consciousness of the requirement for economical practices, are fundamental to relieving the natural impression of the 4IR.

With regards to international affairs, the Fourth Modern Upheaval presents new elements and difficulties. The race for mechanical predominance, especially in regions like artificial intelligence and quantum figuring, has suggestions for monetary seriousness and public safety. The moral contemplations encompassing the turn of events and sending of cutting edge innovations highlight the requirement for worldwide participation and the foundation of moral norms to direct the worldwide local area in exploring the difficulties of the 4IR.

The Fourth Modern Unrest is definitely not a solid power yet a mind boggling transaction of innovations, cultural changes, and financial changes. Its direction is formed by human decisions, strategies, and the aggregate reaction to challenges. Embracing the chances of the 4IR requires an all encompassing methodology that thinks about the moral, social, and financial components of mechanical advancement.

All in all, the Fourth Modern Unrest addresses a urgent crossroads in mankind's set of experiences, where the limits between the physical, computerized, and organic domains are obscured. The extraordinary effect of advancements like computer based intelligence, IoT, and mechanical technology is reshaping ventures, reclassifying the idea of work, and impacting each aspect of human existence. Exploring the difficulties and chances of the 4IR requires an aggregate and ground breaking approach that focuses on moral contemplations, natural manageability, and inclusivity. As the excursion into the Fourth Modern Transformation unfurls, humankind remains at the intersection of extraordinary mechanical potential and the obligation to shape a future that is both creative and impartial.

1.2 Historical Milestones in Automation

The direction of robotization is set apart by a progression of verifiable achievements that mirror humankind's determined quest for proficiency, development, and mechanical headway. From the earliest mechanical gadgets to the modern frameworks of the current day, the development of robotization is a demonstration of our resourcefulness and our mission to expand and, on occasion, supplant human work with mechanical and computerized partners.

The starting points of robotization can be followed back to antiquated developments, where simple apparatuses were made to improve on manual errands. The development of the wheel, for instance, was an essential move toward mechanizing the development of merchandise. Straightforward machines like pulleys and switches additionally arose, displaying the early comprehension of mechanical rules that would later support more complicated mechanized frameworks.

The Medieval times saw the advancement of mechanical tickers, a development that added to the normalization of timekeeping. These multifaceted gadgets, driven by cog wheels and loads, showed an early type of computerized hardware intended to carry out a particular role. As social orders embraced exchange and trade, the requirement for exact timekeeping turned out to be progressively basic, featuring the down to earth utilizations of mechanization.

The Renaissance time saw the formation of automata, mechanical gadgets intended to impersonate human or creature developments. These complicated perfect timing figures, frequently displayed in imperial courts, were wonders of designing and craftsmanship. While principally filling in as diversion, automata laid the preparation for future headways in mechanical technology and the mechanization of perplexing developments.

The Modern Unrest, crossing the late eighteenth to the mid nineteenth hundreds of years, addresses a turning point throughout the entire existence of computerization. Steam power, outfit through the innovation of the steam motor, changed ventures by giving another wellspring of energy. Plants arose as the focal point of creation, and the motorization of material assembling turned into an image of the transformation's effect on work and productivity.

The mid twentieth century saw the coming of sequential construction system creation, an advancement credited to Henry Passage in the car business. By separating the assembling system into a grouping of redundant undertakings, the mechanical production system decisively expanded proficiency and brought down creation costs. This change in outlook in assembling denoted the progress from high quality craftsmanship to large scale manufacturing, making way for the normalization of products.

The 1930s saw the presentation of the main electronic PC, the Atanasoff-Berry PC (ABC), created by John Atanasoff and Clifford Berry. Albeit simple by current norms, the ABC laid the foundation for the advanced figuring upheaval that would follow. The resulting many years saw the rise of centralized server PCs, preparing for the robotization of complicated computations and information handling.

The 1950s and 1960s saw the improvement of the primary modern robots. Unimate, presented in 1961, is many times credited as the principal economically accessible automated framework. Created by George

Devol and Joseph Engelberger, Unimate was at first conveyed in a General Engines production line for material dealing with undertakings. This obvious the start of the coordination of mechanical technology into assembling processes, flagging another period in mechanization.

The late twentieth century saw the far and wide reception of programmable rationale regulators (PLCs) in modern settings. These particular computerized PCs were intended to control fabricating cycles and hardware. Their adaptability and dependability made them a foundation of computerization in businesses going from auto assembling to food handling. PLCs keep on assuming a vital part in modern computerization right up to the present day.

The appearance of chip and PCs during the 1970s and 1980s democratized registering power, making it more available to people and independent ventures. This shift established the groundwork for the computerization of office assignments, with the improvement of programming applications that smoothed out regulatory cycles, going from word handling to monetary estimations.

The late twentieth century additionally saw the ascent of modern robotization frameworks known as Administrative Control and Information Obtaining (SCADA). SCADA frameworks took into consideration the incorporated observing and control of modern cycles, upgrading effectiveness and empowering constant navigation. These frameworks became vital in areas like energy, water treatment, and assembling.

The joining of robotization into the field of broadcast communications introduced another time of network. The advancement of programmed phone trades and the development towards computerized correspondence networks worked with the computerization of telecom processes. The web, a result of continuous computerization in data trade, arose as a worldwide organization that changed correspondence, business, and admittance to data.

The turn of the 21st century saw the assembly of computerization with man-made reasoning (artificial intelligence). AI calculations, fit for gaining from information and further developing execution over the long haul, turned out to be progressively refined. This simulated intelligence driven robotization tracked down applications in assorted fields, from picture and discourse acknowledgment to proposal frameworks and independent vehicles.

The ascent of the Web of Things (IoT) in the 21st century denoted a change in perspective in mechanization. The interconnection of ordinary gadgets inserted with sensors and programming empowered the consistent trade of information. Savvy homes, furnished with IoT gadgets, considered remote observing and control of different family capabilities, epitomizing the mix of mechanization into day to day existence.

The improvement of independent vehicles, especially in the car and aviation businesses, displayed the capability of computerization to upset transportation. Self-driving vehicles, robots, and, surprisingly, trial projects like Hyperloop indicated a future where machines could explore complex conditions independently, testing conventional ideas of human-controlled transportation.

Progressions in biotechnology and medical care computerization significantly affect clinical diagnostics and therapy. Mechanized research center gear, mechanical medical procedure frameworks, and computer based intelligence controlled analytic apparatuses have improved the accuracy and effectiveness of medical services conveyance. The Fourth Modern Upheaval has delivered the possibility of customized medication, where medicines are custom-made to a person's hereditary cosmetics.

The development of robotization in agribusiness, frequently alluded to as accuracy cultivating, has changed customary cultivating rehearses. Mechanized apparatus, furnished with GPS innovation and sensors, can streamline planting, collecting, and water system processes. This increments productivity as well as adds to maintainable farming by limiting asset use and natural effect.

The Fourth Modern Upset is described by the combination of digital actual frameworks, simulated intelligence, and the Web of Things, leading to the idea of Industry 4.0. Brilliant industrial facilities, empowered by associated gadgets and savvy computerization, plan to improve creation processes, upgrade adaptability, and empower prescient support. The vision of Industry 4.0 addresses an all encompassing way to deal with computerization, underscoring the combination of advanced innovations across the whole worth chain.

The improvement of quantum registering, with the possibility to take care of mind boggling issues at speeds impossible by traditional PCs, adds another aspect to the scene of robotization. Quantum PCs, when acknowledged at scale, could change fields like cryptography, streamlining, and reenactment, opening up conceivable outcomes that were once remembered to be past the scope of computational innovation.

As robotization keeps on propelling, the moral ramifications of man-made intelligence and AI become progressively unmistakable. The choices made via mechanized frameworks, especially in touchy spaces like law enforcement, medical services, and money, bring up issues about responsibility, straightforwardness, and predisposition.

The moral contemplations encompassing computerization highlight the significance of dependable turn of events and organization of these innovations.

1.3 Automation's Impact on Employment Trends

The unyielding walk of robotization, impelled by headways in advanced mechanics, computerized reasoning (man-made intelligence), and advanced innovations, has essentially reshaped business patterns across different ventures. The effect of computerization on positions has been a subject of conversation and worry, as the groundbreaking force of innovation meets with the elements of the worldwide labor force. Understanding what robotization means for business patterns requires an investigation of its diverse impacts on work creation, work uprooting, and the developing idea of work.

One of the focal parts of mechanization's effect on work is the robotization of normal, dreary undertakings. Businesses like assembling, where tedious and unsurprising errands are pervasive, have seen an eminent shift towards robotization. Mechanical arms, mechanized sequential construction systems, and AI calculations have assumed control over errands that were once performed by human laborers. While this has prompted expanded effectiveness, diminished blunders, and lower creation costs, it has likewise brought about the relocation of specific positions.

The assembling area, generally a significant boss, has gone through huge changes because of robotization. Customary plant occupations, especially those including manual get together and routine cycles, have seen a decay. All things considered, there is a developing interest for laborers with abilities in working, keeping up with, and programming computerized frameworks. The development of blue collar positions mirrors the more extensive pattern of robotization not taking out positions however changing the abilities expected for work in a given industry.

The coming of Industry 4.0, portrayed by the coordination of digital actual frameworks, IoT, and artificial intelligence in assembling, has additionally strengthened the interest for a labor force with computerized education and specific abilities. Occupations in savvy plants include working with information examination, programming PLCs, and managing the activity of interconnected frameworks. The changing idea of assembling business features the significance of upskilling and reskilling for laborers to stay pertinent in an undeniably mechanized scene.

Past assembling, robotization has made critical advances into areas like retail, coordinated operations, and client assistance. Computerized checkout frameworks in grocery stores, self-administration stands in retail locations, and robotized distribution centers outfitted with mechanical pickers are instances of how mechanization is changing the essence of customary retail and planned operations. While these advances upgrade functional effectiveness, they likewise influence occupations connected with cashiering, stock administration, and manual request picking.

The ascent of web based business and the reception of mechanized frameworks in satisfaction communities have prompted a flood popular for laborers with abilities in overseeing and keeping up with these advances. Occupations in planned operations presently require capability in taking care of robotized stock frameworks, organizing with independent vehicles, and investigating mechanical errors. The joining of robotization in retail and coordinated factors highlights the significance of flexibility despite mechanical change.

Client assistance is another area where mechanization has taken critical steps. Chatbots, menial helpers, and computerized tagging frameworks have become typical in tending to client questions and issues. While these advances offer all day, every day accessibility and speedy reactions, they likewise influence occupations in conventional call places and client assistance jobs. The developing scene of client care work requests a shift towards jobs that include planning, executing, and directing computerized client cooperation frameworks.

In the domain of expert administrations, robotization has started to assume a groundbreaking part. The coming of man-made intelligence fueled devices for information examination, lawful exploration, and monetary demonstrating has smoothed out errands that were customarily done by human experts. While mechanization in proficient administrations can possibly increment effectiveness and lessen costs, it likewise prompts a reexamination of the abilities expected in these callings. The capacity to use and decipher information, figure out man-made intelligence calculations, and spotlight on complex critical thinking becomes urgent in a scene where routine errands are mechanized.

The effect of robotization isn't bound to normal and manual undertakings; it reaches out to scholarly errands that include design acknowledgment, information examination, and independent direction. AI calculations, equipped for handling tremendous measures of information and distinguishing designs, have found applications in different fields like money, medical care, and promoting. Computerized dynamic cycles, driven by calculations, have suggestions for work jobs that include routine direction in light of predefined rules.

The monetary business gives an illustrative illustration of how robotization plays penetrated parts generally held by human experts. Algorithmic exchanging, robo-counsels, and mechanized risk evaluation instruments have become essential parts of monetary administrations. While these advances offer proficiency and accuracy in monetary activities, they likewise bring up issues about the job of human judgment, moral contemplations in algorithmic navigation, and the requirement for administrative structures to guarantee straightforwardness and responsibility.

In medical services, mechanization has affected different viewpoints, from analytic cycles to regulatory undertakings. Computer based intelligence driven symptomatic devices, clinical imaging examination, and automated helped medical procedures have improved the precision

and effectiveness of medical care conveyance. In any case, the joining of robotization in medical care likewise presents difficulties, especially in dealing with the moral ramifications of computer based intelligence in conclusion and therapy choices. Medical services experts presently end up working close by robotized frameworks, requiring a mix of specialized capability and relational abilities.

The rising predominance of computerization in different areas highlights the significance of a dynamic and versatile labor force. While specific positions face uprooting because of computerization, new jobs arise, frequently requiring abilities in fields like information science, programming, network protection, and advanced education. The advancement of business patterns in the time of computerization requires a proactive way to deal with training and expertise improvement to outfit people with the devices expected to flourish in a quickly changing position market.

The idea of the gig economy, described by present moment, independent, or self employed entity commitment, has acquired noticeable quality with regards to robotization. Innovation stages that associate specialists with undertakings or ventures have prospered, offering adaptability and independence. Gig work frequently includes undertakings that are challenging to robotize, like imaginative work, individual administrations, or jobs that require a serious level of flexibility. In any case, the gig economy additionally raises worries about professional stability, specialist benefits, and the requirement for administrative systems to address the novel difficulties of this business model.

The convergence of computerization and the gig economy features the significance of encouraging a different range of abilities that incorporates imagination, the capacity to understand individuals on a profound level, and versatility. Occupations that include complex critical thinking, decisive reasoning, and inventive articulation are less defenseless to mechanization. The accentuation on delicate abilities becomes vital as mechanization assumes control over routine errands, passing on people to zero in on extraordinarily human capacities that machines can't duplicate.

The advancement of business patterns in the time of mechanization not set in stone by the substitution of occupations; it is additionally molded by the making of new open doors and the change of existing jobs. The idea of human-machine joint effort acquires conspicuousness, stressing the corresponding idea of human and machine capacities. Instead of survey computerization as a danger, a cooperative methodology imagines a future where people and machines cooperate to accomplish results that neither could achieve freely.

The job of policymakers, teachers, and industry pioneers becomes significant in exploring the difficulties and potential open doors introduced via robotization. Policymakers are entrusted with making administrative structures that offset advancement with contemplations of occupation uprooting, specialist privileges, and moral utilization of innovation.

Schooling systems should adjust to furnish people with the abilities expected in a mechanized scene, underlining decisive reasoning, versatility, and advanced education.

The effect of computerization on work patterns isn't uniform across all areas and locales. While certain enterprises experience work removal, others witness a flood popular for talented laborers in arising fields. Geological and financial elements assume a part in molding the differential effect of computerization on networks. Spanning the advanced separation and guaranteeing fair admittance to instructive open doors are fundamental stages in encouraging comprehensive development in the time of robotization.

The direction of business patterns in the time of mechanization is entwined with more extensive cultural contemplations. The idea of widespread essential pay, a type of government backed retirement that gives people a customary, unqualified amount of cash, has acquired consideration as a possible reaction to the difficulties presented via mechanization prompted work relocation. While the thought plans to address monetary disparity and give a security net notwithstanding changing business elements, it likewise prompts banters about its possibility, financial ramifications, and expected cultural effect.

1.4 Ethical Considerations in Automation

The fast progressions in robotization advances, driven by man-made brainpower (man-made intelligence), AI, and mechanical technology, have introduced a period where machines assume an undeniably basic part in direction, day to day errands, and different parts of human existence. As mechanization penetrates different areas, moral contemplations become vital. The moral ramifications of computerization address issues of responsibility, straightforwardness, inclination, security, and the more extensive cultural effect of these advances.

One of the essential moral worries in mechanization rotates around the responsibility for choices made via computerized frameworks. As machines, especially those controlled by simulated intelligence, settle on choices in settings going from money to law enforcement, questions emerge about who bears liability when these choices lead to potentially negative side-effects or damage. Laying out clear lines of responsibility becomes testing when calculations and mechanized processes are involved, as they miss the mark on awareness and moral organization innate in human chiefs.

The absence of straightforwardness in computerized dynamic cycles further muddles the issue of responsibility. Numerous man-made intelligence and AI calculations work as "secret elements," meaning the internal functions of the framework are not promptly reasonable or logical. This haziness raises worries about how choices are reached, what variables impact those choices, and whether predispositions are incidentally propagated inside the framework. Guaranteeing straightforwardness is significant to encouraging confidence in computerized frameworks and considering them responsible for their activities.

Predisposition in computerized frameworks is an unavoidable moral worry that has gathered expanding consideration. AI calculations gain from verifiable information, and on the off chance that this information contains predispositions, the calculations might propagate or try and worsen those predispositions in their dynamic cycles. This is especially apparent in applications, for example, employing processes, where one-sided preparing information can prompt unfair results. Tending to predisposition in computerization requires cautious thought of the information used to prepare calculations and progressing endeavors to distinguish and amend inclinations in framework yields.

Security is one more moral aspect that is significantly affected via robotization. As robotized frameworks gather, process, and examine immense measures of information, concerns emerge about the security of people's protection. Reconnaissance advances, computerized facial acknowledgment, and information mining rehearses bring up issues about the limits among public and confidential spaces and the potential for mass observation. Adjusting the advantages of robotization with the need to shield individual protection privileges is a sensitive moral test.

The moral contemplations in robotization reach out into the domain of work and the financial effect of occupation dislodging. While mechanization achieves expanded effectiveness and efficiency, it likewise raises worries about the possible loss of occupations, especially those including standard and dreary assignments. The moral basic lies in dealing with the progress to a computerized labor force in a manner that limits the adverse consequence on people and networks. This might include drives for reskilling, upskilling, and setting out new open doors in arising ventures.

Robotization likewise converges with moral contemplations with regards to the gig economy. The utilization of computerized stages to associate specialists with present moment or independent errands presents inquiries regarding professional stability, fair pay, and laborer freedoms. Guaranteeing moral work rehearses in the gig economy requires a cautious assessment of the connections between laborers, stages, and businesses to forestall double-dealing and maintain the nobility and prosperity of laborers.

The moral utilization of robotization in medical care is a basic thought given the delicate idea of clinical information and patient consideration. Man-made intelligence applications in clinical finding, treatment arranging, and mechanical helped medical procedures hold enormous commitment for further developing medical care results. Notwithstanding, worries about the security of wellbeing information, the potential for one-sided calculations, and the requirement for human oversight in clinical dynamic highlight the significance of moral rules and guidelines in the medical care area.

The organization of independent frameworks, like self-driving vehicles and robots, presents moral contemplations in the domain of security. Choices made by these frameworks in certifiable situations should focus on the prosperity of people and networks.

Adjusting the expected advantages of independent frameworks, like diminished car crashes, with the moral basic to limit hurt in unanticipated circumstances requires a complete way to deal with security guidelines and guidelines.

The moral elements of robotization are additionally apparent in the military and guard area. The utilization of independent weapons, fit for pursuing deadly choices without direct human mediation, brings up significant moral issues. Issues of responsibility, adherence to worldwide compassionate regulation, and the potential for unseen side-effects in the utilization of deadly independent frameworks brief worldwide conversations about the moral furthest reaches of computerization in military applications.

As robotization innovations advance, the moral contemplations encompassing the turn of events and sending of fake general insight (AGI) come to the very front. AGI addresses a type of knowledge that could outperform human capacities across a great many undertakings. The moral difficulties presented by AGI remember worries about its effect for work, the potential for it to dominate human control, and the existential dangers related with exceptionally independent frameworks. Guaranteeing moral rules and shields in AGI advancement becomes pivotal to relieve dangers and guide the dependable arrangement of such strong advancements.

The idea of "logic" in artificial intelligence frameworks is key to tending to moral worries about straightforwardness and responsibility. As artificial intelligence calculations go with choices that influence people's lives, the capacity to comprehend and make sense of the thinking behind those choices becomes fundamental. Reasonable computer based intelligence expects to demystify the dynamic course of calculations, giving experiences into how they come to explicit end results. This straightforwardness encourages trust, empowers responsibility, and considers the ID and amendment of inclinations.

The moral contemplations in mechanization likewise stretch out to the natural effect of mechanical headways. The energy utilization related with server farms, fabricating processes, and the removal of electronic waste brings up issues about the supportability of computerization.

The turn of events and reception of green advancements, alongside the execution of naturally cognizant practices, are fundamental to relieving the biological impression of mechanization.

The job of moral plan standards in the advancement of mechanized frameworks couldn't possibly be more significant. Guaranteeing that advancements are planned in view of moral contemplations, from the beginning phases of improvement to organization, is a proactive way to deal with tending to expected moral difficulties. Moral plan includes thinking about the social, social, and moral ramifications of advances, expecting to make frameworks that line up with human qualities and contribute emphatically to society.

Tending to moral contemplations in robotization requires a multi-disciplinary approach that includes cooperation between technologists, ethicists, policymakers, and the more extensive public. Laying out clear moral rules, creating mindful computer based intelligence systems, and taking part in open discoursed about the cultural effect of robotization are fundamental stages in exploring the moral intricacies of these advances.

All in all, the moral contemplations in mechanization are natural for the mindful turn of events and sending of advances that undeniably shape our day to day routines. From guaranteeing straightforwardness and responsibility to tending to inclination and safeguarding individual security, moral contemplations give a structure to exploring the intricate scene of mechanization. As society wrestles with the groundbreaking effect of robotization, cultivating a moral methodology becomes basic to saddle the advantages of innovation while defending central qualities and standards.

A basic part of tending to moral contemplations in mechanization includes the improvement of strong administrative structures. The quick speed of mechanical progression frequently exceeds the capacity of existing guidelines to keep up. Policymakers face the test of making regulations that find some kind of harmony between cultivating devel-opment and shielding moral standards. Administrative measures might incorporate rules for dependable computer based intelligence advancement, systems for information assurance, and norms for the moral utilization of mechanization in different areas.

The cooperative work to lay out moral guidelines stretches out to industry partners and expert associations. Tech organizations, specialists, and engineers assume a urgent part in molding the moral scene of robotization. Industry-explicit sets of principles, best practices, and moral rules add to an aggregate obligation to capable development. Moral contemplations ought to be necessary to the whole lifecycle of an innovation, from its origination and plan to its organization and progressing use.

Schooling and mindfulness drives are fundamental parts of tending to moral contemplations in robotization. As innovative proficiency turns out to be progressively pivotal, teaching the general population about the moral ramifications of mechanization engages people to pursue informed choices. Public talk, educated by an exhaustive comprehension regarding the moral components of innovation, adds to the improvement of cultural standards and assumptions.

Worldwide participation is essential in tending to the worldwide idea of moral difficulties in mechanization. Given the borderless idea of innovation and its effect, cooperative endeavors among countries are important to lay out normal moral principles. Gatherings for worldwide exchange, settlements on moral rules, and participation on innovative work can add to a mutual perspective of capable robotization rehearses on a worldwide scale.

The standard of reasonableness in computerization requests consideration regarding issues of value and incorporation. Guaranteeing that mechanized frameworks don't worsen existing cultural disparities is a center moral thought. This includes tending to predispositions in calculations, advancing variety in the advancement of innovation, and taking into account the more extensive social ramifications of mechanized direction. Moral structures should effectively make progress toward making frameworks that are fair and only for all citizenry.

The idea of "significant worth arrangement" is essential to moral contemplations in robotization. Esteem arrangement includes guaranteeing that computerized frameworks line up with human qualities, standards, and cultural objectives. Understanding and integrating different viewpoints, social settings, and moral structures into the improvement of mechanization innovations makes frameworks that regard and mirror the upsides of the networks they serve. Esteem arrangement additionally includes expecting and tending to likely contentions between the qualities implanted in robotized frameworks and those of people or networks.

In the domain of occupation relocation because of robotization, moral contemplations stretch out to the obligation of businesses and policymakers to deal with the cultural effect. Drives, for example, reskilling and upskilling programs, support for dislodged laborers, and the production of new business open doors add to a moral way to deal with the changing idea of work. Moral contemplations stress a pledge to limiting the unfortunate results of robotization on business and guaranteeing a simply change for impacted people.

The moral contemplations in the gig economy expect regard for the privileges and prosperity of gig laborers. Fair remuneration, admittance to advantages, and security from double-dealing are major moral contemplations in the gig economy. Administrative structures that balance the adaptability of gig work with the requirement for laborer securities assume a significant part in maintaining moral principles in this developing business model.

In medical services, where robotization advancements can possibly fundamentally affect patient consideration, moral rules are fundamental. Safeguarding patient security, guaranteeing educated assent for the utilization regarding computerized instruments, and keeping a harmony among innovation and human-focused care are focal moral contemplations. The Hippocratic guideline of "cause no damage" takes on new importance as computerization innovations become necessary to clinical finding, treatment, and direction.

The moral utilization of mechanization in schooling includes contemplations connected with information protection, value, and the effect on learning results. Mechanized reviewing frameworks, man-made intelligence driven mentoring, and customized learning stages bring up issues about how information is utilized, the potential for building up instructive variations, and the requirement for a human-driven way to deal with schooling. Moral rules in schooling ought to focus on the prosperity of understudies, the impartial dissemination of assets, and the cultivating of decisive reasoning abilities.

Moral contemplations in the turn of events and sending of independent frameworks, like self-driving vehicles and robots, require an emphasis on security, responsibility, and cultural effect. Guaranteeing that independent frameworks focus on the wellbeing of people and networks is a crucial moral objective. Laying out clear rules for dependable use, leading exhaustive gamble appraisals, and tending to public worries about the expected dangers and advantages of independent advancements add to a moral methodology in this area.

The moral contemplations encompassing the utilization of independent weapons in the military require cautious assessment of standards connected with human control, proportionality, and adherence to worldwide helpful regulation. The "deadly independence" of machines brings up significant moral issues about the moral furthest reaches of mechanization in fighting. Global endeavors to lay out deals and arrangements that oversee the utilization of independent weapons expect to forestall the advancement of innovations that could present critical moral and helpful dangers.

The existential dangers related with the improvement of fake general knowledge (AGI) brief moral contemplations that stretch out past quick applications. Shielding against the potentially negative side-effects of exceptionally independent frameworks requires a proactive way to deal with moral rules and hazard relief. The idea of "significant worth arrangement" turns out to be especially urgent while thinking about the expected effects of AGI on cultural designs, human qualities, and the protection of human organization.

The moral contemplations in mechanization additionally meet with more extensive cultural inquiries concerning the effect of innovation on majority rules system, basic freedoms, and the circulation of force. The job of robotization in forming public talk, impacting political cycles, and working with reconnaissance raises moral worries about the convergence of force in the possession of a couple. Moral structures should address the cultural ramifications of mechanical progressions and work towards guaranteeing that the advantages of robotization are conveyed impartially.

As computerization advances keep on developing, moral contemplations become dynamic and complex. The continuous discourse about the moral ramifications of computerization requires versatility and responsiveness to arising difficulties. Research, interdisciplinary joint effort, and a guarantee to consistent moral reflection are fundamental parts of exploring the developing scene of mechanization in a mindful and honest way.

All in all, moral contemplations in robotization are necessary to molding a future where innovation lines up with human qualities, encourages cultural prosperity, and maintains basic standards. From responsibility and straightforwardness to decency and worth arrangement, moral systems give direction to the mindful turn of events and sending of mechanization innovations.

The continuous quest for moral greatness in computerization requires an aggregate responsibility from technologists, policymakers, teachers, and society on the loose to guarantee that the groundbreaking force of robotization contributes emphatically to the headway of humankind.

Chapter 2

The Shifting Workforce Landscape

The contemporary labor force scene is going through a significant change, formed by an intersection of innovative progressions, segment moves, and developing cultural perspectives towards work. This transformation has introduced a time where conventional business models are being re-imagined, and the actual idea of work is going through a seismic shift. As we explore this unique territory, it becomes basic to comprehend the key drivers that are reshaping the labor force scene and the ramifications they hold for people, organizations, and society at large.

One of the essential impetuses for change is the steady walk of innovation. The computerized upset, portrayed by the quick multiplication of computerization, man-made reasoning (simulated intelligence), and high level advanced mechanics, is essentially adjusting the abilities expected in the labor force. Standard and dull undertakings are progressively being robotized, prompting an interest for a more different range of abilities that incorporates critical thinking, inventiveness, and flexibility. As machines take on routine errands, people are freed to zero in on higher-request mental capabilities that machines presently battle to recreate.

This change in ability necessities is reshaping the schooling and preparing scene. Conventional instructive models, intended for a modern period economy, are being examined for their pertinence in reality as we know it where the half-existence of abilities is decreasing quickly. Deep rooted learning is arising as a basic part of vocation achievement, as need might arise to consistently obtain new abilities to remain important in a unique work market. This has led to a flood in web based learning stages, miniature credentialing, and other adaptable learning models that empower people to upskill or reskill at their own speed and according to their own preferences.

Besides, the gig economy, portrayed by present moment and independent work game plans, is acquiring noticeable quality as an option in contrast to customary business models. Empowered by advanced stages that interface laborers with managers, the gig economy offers adaptability and independence to laborers, permitting them to pick when and where they work. This shift towards contemporary work game plans has suggestions for professional stability, benefits, and the general common agreement among bosses and representatives.

Segment changes are likewise assuming a urgent part in molding the labor force scene. The maturing populace in many created nations is prompting a developing interest for medical care and social administrations, setting out open doors in these areas. All the while, more youthful ages entering the labor force bring an alternate arrangement of values and assumptions, impacting work environment culture and elements. The intergenerational variety in the labor force requires a nuanced way to deal with the board and coordinated effort, as various age gatherings might have unmistakable inclinations and workstyles.

The geological conveyance of the labor force is likewise developing, on account of progressions in remote work advancements. The Coronavirus pandemic filled in as an impetus, speeding up the reception of remote work and testing the conventional idea of the working environment. Thus, numerous associations are reconsidering their way to deal with remote work, with some taking on half and half models that mix face to face and remote work game plans. This shift has significant ramifications for urbanization, as laborers are not generally fastened to downtown areas, possibly prompting a reallocation of ability and monetary movement.

In this period of quick change, versatility and nimbleness are becoming key differentiators for the two people and associations. The capacity to turn, embrace change, and master new abilities rapidly is fundamental for remaining cutthroat in an unstable work market. For organizations, developing a culture of advancement and constant learning is essential for drawing in and holding top ability. The customary vocation stepping stool is being supplanted by a cross section, where horizontal moves, expertise improvement, and different encounters are esteemed as much as, while possibly not more than, vertical movement.

Nonetheless, the moving labor force scene isn't without its difficulties. Pay imbalance, exacerbated by the gig economy and the tricky idea of some contemporary work plans, is a squeezing concern. Admittance to quality schooling and preparing open doors isn't uniform, making variations in that frame of mind of people to adjust to the changing expertise necessities of the gig market. Besides, the disintegration of professional stability in the gig economy brings up issues about the social wellbeing net and the eventual fate of business related advantages, for example, medical services and retirement plans.

The job of state run administrations in exploring these progressions is critical. Policymakers are defied with the assignment of planning structures that balance adaptability and assurance for laborers, guaranteeing that the advantages of innovative progressions are impartially conveyed. Drives to advance schooling and preparing, especially for those in danger of being abandoned, are fundamental. Also, reconsidering social security nets to oblige the advancing idea of work is fundamental for address the difficulties presented by pay instability and occupation weakness.

Business pioneers, as well, play an essential part to play in forming the labor force representing things to come. The accentuation on moral man-made intelligence and mindful robotization is getting some decent forward movement, as associations wrestle with the ramifications of sending advancements that could dislodge human specialists. Developing a corporate culture that values variety, value, and consideration isn't just an ethical goal yet in addition a competitive edge in a globalized and interconnected world. Organizations that focus on representative prosperity, give potential open doors to consistent learning, and cultivate a feeling of direction are bound to draw in and hold top ability.

The eventual fate of work is complicatedly attached to the more extensive cultural and monetary setting. As we witness the unfurling of the Fourth Modern Unrest, portrayed by the combination of advanced, natural, and actual innovations, the lines between the physical and virtual universes are obscuring. This union is reshaping enterprises, making new plans of action, and rethinking the actual idea of what is work.

The ascent of stage based organizations, filled by information and network, is upsetting conventional enterprises and setting out new open doors for development. From ride-sharing stages to independent commercial centers, these computerized environments are changing how labor and products are delivered, conveyed, and consumed. The gig economy, a sign of this computerized disturbance, is meaningful of the shift towards a more decentralized and adaptable work market.

Blockchain innovation, with its capability to make straightforward and sealed frameworks, is ready to affect the idea of work in different areas. Savvy contracts, fueled by blockchain, could robotize and uphold authoritative arrangements, smoothing out cycles and decreasing the requirement for middle people. This has suggestions for ventures like money, regulation, and store network the executives, where trust and straightforwardness are principal.

The appearance of 5G innovation is another distinct advantage, empowering quicker and more dependable correspondence. This works with the inescapable reception of distant advancements, increased and computer generated reality, and the Web of Things (IoT). The capacity to associate and control gadgets progressively opens up opportunities for remote work, brilliant urban communities, and a large group of uses that were recently obliged by data transmission restrictions.

Man-made reasoning, frequently hailed as the foundation of the Fourth Modern Upset, is reshaping the labor force in significant ways. AI calculations are becoming capable at performing undertakings that were once selective to human insight, from picture acknowledgment to normal language handling. While this presents amazing open doors for proficiency and advancement, it likewise raises moral worries about work removal and the cultural effect of far reaching computerization.

The moral contemplations encompassing simulated intelligence and mechanization reach out past work uprooting to inquiries of inclination, responsibility, and straightforwardness. As calculations progressively impact dynamic in regions, for example, recruiting, loaning, and law enforcement, guaranteeing decency and forestalling separation turns into a principal concern. Finding some kind of harmony among development and moral protections is a complicated test that requires coordinated effort between technologists, policymakers, and ethicists.

Network protection is one more basic component of the developing labor force scene. As associations embrace computerized change, the volume of information being produced and traded increments dramatically. This information, frequently containing delicate data, turns into a rewarding objective for digital dangers. Safeguarding the respectability of computerized frameworks and the protection of people is a steady fight, requiring progressing interests in network safety measures and a proactive way to deal with moderating dangers.

The interconnectedness of the worldwide economy further intensifies the effect of these innovative movements. The capacity to team up across borders, worked with by computerized stages and correspondence innovations, is making a really worldwide labor force. This globalization presents the two potential open doors and difficulties, as organizations explore social contrasts, administrative structures, and international pressures. The opposition for ability is not generally restricted to nearby or public limits, heightening the requirement for associations to construct different and comprehensive groups that can flourish in a worldwide setting.

The fate of work is additionally interwoven with the more extensive talk on maintainability. The ecological effect of customary methods of creation and utilization is provoking a reexamination of strategic policies.

2.1 Skill Trends in the Automated Era

In the consistently advancing scene of work, the appearance of the mechanized period is reshaping the abilities that are considered fundamental for proficient achievement. As robotization, man-made reasoning (computer based intelligence), and trend setting innovations become more unavoidable, the interest for explicit ranges of abilities is going through a significant change. In this time of fast mechanical headway, remaining important in the gig market requires a nuanced comprehension of arising expertise patterns and a guarantee to nonstop learning.

One of the preeminent abilities that has acquired noticeable quality in the computerized time is advanced education. As innovation turns out to be progressively coordinated into different parts of work, from correspondence to information investigation, an essential degree of computerized capability is at this point not a simple benefit yet an essential. Advanced proficiency incorporates the capacity to explore computerized stages, use efficiency instruments, and comprehend essential ideas connected with data innovation. People who can bridle the force of advanced devices are better situated to adjust to the changing idea of work and influence innovation for upgraded efficiency.

Lined up with computerized proficiency, information education has arisen as a basic expertise in the period of robotization. The expansion of information in the present advanced scene requires the capacity to examine, decipher, and get experiences from complex datasets. Information driven navigation is turning into the standard across different businesses, and people who have the right stuff to work with information are popular. This remembers capability for information representation, measurable examination, and the capacity to make significant inferences from assorted datasets. As organizations progressively depend on information to drive key drives, information proficiency turns into a significant resource for experts across disciplines.

Coding and programming abilities are central in the mechanized period, rising above their relationship with conventional IT jobs. The capacity to compose code is not generally bound to programming designers; it has turned into an important expertise for experts in fields as different as promoting, money, and medical services. Coding capability empowers people to mechanize tedious undertakings, examine information all the more successfully, and add to the turn of events and execution of innovative arrangements. Figuring out programming dialects, for example, Python or JavaScript, enables people to draw in with innovation at a more profound level, cultivating development and proficiency.

Decisive reasoning and critical thinking abilities are ageless skills that gain new importance with regards to robotization. As normal undertakings are computerized, the human labor force is progressively entrusted with taking care of mind boggling issues and pursuing vital choices. Decisive reasoning includes the capacity to examine data, assess choices, and make good decisions.

A mental expertise rises above unambiguous businesses and occupation jobs, making it a foundation of flexibility in the computerized period. Experts who can explore uncertainty, think fundamentally, and devise creative arrangements are strategically situated to flourish in a climate where robotization handles routine undertakings.

Inventiveness is arising as a particularly human expertise that supplements the capacities of computerization. While machines succeed at dreary and rule-based errands, inventiveness stays a remarkably human quality. The capacity to think imaginatively, create clever thoughts, and move toward difficulties with advancement is progressively esteemed in the working environment. Whether in the domains of item configuration, promoting, or critical thinking, people who can saddle their imaginative potential add to a culture of development that separates associations in a cutthroat scene. Imagination, joined with computerized education, frames an intense blend for experts trying to explore the robotized time.

Flexibility and a development outlook are fundamental credits for people confronting the vulnerabilities of the robotized time. The speed of mechanical change implies that new devices and cycles will persistently arise, expecting experts to rapidly adjust. A receptiveness to learning, a readiness to embrace change, and a confidence in one's capacity to foster new abilities are parts of a development outlook. In a time where work jobs are developing, and the expertise necessities are dynamic, people with a development outlook are better prepared to explore changes, upskill on a case by case basis, and immediately jump all over chances for professional success.

The capacity to understand people on a profound level (EI) is earning respect as a fundamental expertise in the robotized time, especially as human-machine collaborations become more predominant. EI incorporates the capacity to comprehend and deal with one's own feelings, as well as explore and impact the feelings of others. In a working environment where joint effort, correspondence, and relational connections are necessary, the capacity to understand people on a profound level adds to powerful cooperation and initiative. As robotization handles routine errands, the human labor force's capacity to interface, sympathize, team up turns into a key differentiator.

Network protection abilities are progressively popular as associations wrestle with the difficulties of getting advanced framework. The ascent of mechanization and the interconnectedness of computerized frameworks enhance the significance of safeguarding delicate information and forestalling digital dangers. Experts with mastery in network protection assume a critical part in defending associations against breaks, guaranteeing the respectability of computerized frameworks, and moderating the dangers related with a developing danger scene. The capacity to comprehend and execute network safety measures is essential to keeping up with the trust and security of computerized conditions.

Interdisciplinary abilities are acquiring noticeable quality as the limits between conventional work jobs obscure in the robotized time. Experts who can connect holes between various disciplines carry an all encompassing viewpoint to critical thinking and development. For instance, people with a blend of specialized abilities and space explicit information, like medical care or money, are strategically situated to contribute genuinely to projects that require a union of mastery. Interdisciplinary joint effort encourages a more all encompassing way to deal with tending to complex difficulties, lining up with the requests of a labor force formed via robotization.

Delicate abilities, enveloping correspondence, cooperation, and relational capacities, remain fundamental in the computerized period. While specialized abilities are essential, the capacity to work successfully with others, impart thoughts obviously, and team up on projects is vital. As mechanization changes the idea of work, the significance of human-driven abilities turns out to be significantly more articulated. Viable correspondence, both composed and verbal, is an expertise that rises above work jobs and ventures, working with coordinated effort and guaranteeing that thoughts are conveyed obviously in a different and interconnected work environment.

Consistent learning and flexibility are individual objectives as well as authoritative needs in the mechanized time. Associations that encourage a culture of learning, give potential open doors to proficient turn of events, and backing workers in getting new abilities are better situated to explore the difficulties of computerization. From formal preparation projects to casual learning drives, establishing a helpful climate for ceaseless expertise improvement is fundamental for remaining serious in a scene where the main steady is change.

All in all, the computerized period carries with it a redefinition of the abilities that are most important in the labor force. While specialized abilities like computerized proficiency, coding, and information investigation are fundamental, they are supplemented by extraordinarily human abilities like decisive reasoning, imagination, the capacity to appreciate individuals at their core, and versatility. The advancing idea of work requests a comprehensive way to deal with expertise improvement that includes both specialized and delicate abilities. As people and associations explore the potential open doors and difficulties of the computerized time, a guarantee to ceaseless learning, a development outlook, and an emphasis on human-driven abilities will be vital to flourishing in the powerful scene of work.

2.2 Job Displacement and Creation Dynamics

Work uprooting and creation elements are at the very front of conversations encompassing the advancing universe of work. The powers of mechanical advancement, globalization, and financial movements are reshaping businesses, influencing existing position, and leading to new open doors. Understanding the elements of occupation removal and creation is significant for policymakers, organizations, and people as they explore the intricacies of a quickly changing position market.

Mechanical progressions, especially in robotization and man-made reasoning, have been huge drivers of occupation dislodging. Robotization, as robots and calculations, is progressively equipped for performing standard and tedious errands more productively than people. This has prompted worries about the expected loss of occupations in areas where robotization is quickly progressing, like assembling, coordinated operations, and client support. The apprehension about mechanical joblessness, where machines supplant human laborers for a huge scope, has incited conversations about the eventual fate of work and the requirement for systems to moderate its likely adverse consequence.

In any case, it's fundamental to perceive that mechanical development uproots occupations as well as makes new ones. The historical backdrop of modern transformations shows that while specific positions might become old, new enterprises and occupations arise, producing business open doors. For instance, the ascent of data innovation in the late twentieth century prompted the production of occupations in programming improvement, network safety, and information examination. Additionally, the continuous advanced transformation is encouraging the development of occupations in fields like man-made reasoning, AI, and computerized promoting.

Globalization is another power adding to the elements of occupation relocation and creation. The interconnectedness of economies implies that organizations can work on a worldwide scale, looking for cost efficiencies and getting to a more extensive ability pool. While globalization has without a doubt prompted the production of new positions in enterprises that advantage from worldwide exchange, it has likewise brought about the removal of specific positions, especially in areas where reevaluating and offshoring are pervasive.

The effect of globalization on work uprooting isn't uniform across ventures or districts. A few areas experience uplifted rivalry, prompting employment misfortunes, while others flourish in a more interconnected and globalized commercial center. Moreover, the geographic convergence of specific ventures can bring about restricted work uprooting, as found in districts vigorously subject to a solitary industry or area that goes through massive changes because of globalization.

The idea of work itself is developing, with a shift towards contemporary and gig economy game plans. While these adaptable work game plans give valuable open doors to independence and different revenue sources, they additionally present difficulties connected with employer stability, advantages, and work privileges. The gig economy, described by present moment and independent work, is changing the business representative relationship and testing conventional models of work.

In the gig economy, stages associate specialists with undertakings or tasks, considering more prominent adaptability as far as when and where work is performed. This adaptability is especially alluring to specific socioeconomics, like consultants, self employed entities, and those looking for parttime or transitory work. In any case, the absence of professional stability and the shortfall of customary business benefits, for example, health care coverage and retirement plans, raise worries about the drawn out manageability and prosperity of people took part in gig work.

Work uprooting and creation elements are additionally affected by segment shifts, remembering changes for populace size, age appropriation, and labor force interest rates. Maturing populaces in many created nations present difficulties and open doors for the work market. On one hand, there is an expanded interest for medical care and eldercare administrations, setting out work open doors in these areas. Then again, the retirement of a huge part of the labor force can prompt abilities deficiencies in specific ventures.

Segment changes additionally add to the development of ability necessities. As more established specialists resign, there is a requirement for a more youthful labor force furnished with abilities pertinent to the requests of the computerized economy. This progress requires interests in schooling and preparing programs that address the arising ability holes. The exchange between segment shifts and innovative headways highlights the significance of adjusting labor force improvement methodologies to the developing requirements of the gig market.

Government strategies assume a critical part in molding position relocation and creation elements. Work market guidelines, exchange approaches, and interests in schooling and preparing projects can impact the flexibility of the labor force despite mechanical disturbances and monetary movements. Strategies that help upskilling and reskilling drives can upgrade the flexibility of the labor force, empowering people to progress to new and arising ventures.

Besides, social wellbeing nets and joblessness benefits become basic components to help people encountering position dislodging. As ventures go through changes, strategies that give a wellbeing net to laborers, for example, joblessness protection and admittance to reasonable medical care, become fundamental for relieving the adverse conse-quence of financial interruptions.

At the hierarchical level, organizations assume a crucial part in dealing with the elements of occupation relocation and creation. Pro-active techniques for labor force arranging, ability advancement, and representative reskilling are fundamental parts of authoritative flexi-bility. Organizations that put resources into the consistent learning and advancement of their labor force are better situated to adjust to mechanical changes and stay cutthroat in powerful business sectors.

Associations can likewise add to work creation by encouraging advancement and investigating new business open doors. The improve-ment of arising innovations, for example, man-made consciousness and environmentally friendly power, opens up new outskirts for organi-zations to

spearhead and make occupations. Besides, a promise to corporate social obligation and economical practices can prompt the making of jobs zeroed in on natural protection, social effect, and moral strategic policies.

People, as well, assume a pivotal part in exploring position uprooting and creation elements. Embracing a mentality of persistent learning and flexibility is fundamental for remaining important in a changing po-sition market. Upskilling and reskilling drives, whether given by bosses or sought after freely, engage people to gain the abilities requested by arising businesses. Building a different range of abilities that consol-idates specialized capability with delicate abilities, for example, corre-spondence and cooperation upgrades one's employability in a unique work market.

Organizing and remaining informed about industry patterns are sig-nificant techniques for people looking to explore work dislodging and creation elements. Participating in proficient networks, going to meet-ings, and partaking in web-based discussions can give bits of knowledge into arising open positions and assist people with situating themselves decisively in the gig market.

The training area is a key participant in setting up the labor force for the difficulties and open doors introduced by work dislodging and creation. Instructive organizations should adjust their educational programs to line up with the advancing requirements of the gig market. Underscoring decisive reasoning, critical thinking, and advanced education furnishes understudies with the central abilities expected for the mechanized period. Cooperation between instructive foundations, industry partners, and policymakers is fundamental to guarantee that schooling and preparing programs are receptive to the requests of a quickly evolving economy.

Taking everything into account, work removal and creation elements are characteristic for the developing idea of work. While mechanical progressions, globalization, and segment shifts add to the removal of specific positions, they likewise set out new open doors in arising ventures. Legislatures, organizations, and people all assume critical parts in forming the reaction to these elements.

Policymakers should plan and carry out techniques that help labor force flexibility, give social security nets, and cultivate the improvement of abilities applicable to the computerized economy. Organizations are entrusted with proactive ability the executives, advancement, and corporate obligation to add to work creation. At the singular level, a guarantee to long lasting learning, versatility, and key situating in the gig market are fundamental for exploring the intricacies of occupation dislodging and creation in a quickly impacting world. The cooperative endeavors of these partners are imperative for making a labor force that is dexterous, talented, and ready for the difficulties and chances representing things to come of work.

2.3 Rethinking Education for an Automated Future

The coming of computerization and man-made brainpower (computer based intelligence) has introduced an extraordinary period that requests a principal reconsidering of instruction. As the idea of work develops, customary schooling models are confronting phenomenal difficulties, requiring a change in outlook to furnish people with the abilities and skills fundamental for progress in a mechanized future. This reexamination includes the educational program as well as the instructive methodologies, learning conditions, and the more extensive way of thinking of training.

One of the focal mainstays of reconsidering training for a robotized future is the accentuation on developing areas of strength for an in computerized education. Advanced education goes past essential PC abilities; it includes the capacity to explore, basically assess, and influence data in a computerized climate. As innovation becomes omnipresent in the working environment, computerized education turns into an essential for viable support in the cutting edge labor force. Instructive educational plans should incorporate advanced proficiency across disciplines, showing understudies how to mindfully utilize innovation, observe believable data from deception, and outfit computerized devices for critical thinking and development.

Coding and programming abilities are progressively perceived as fundamental parts of contemporary instruction. The capacity to comprehend and compose code isn't bound to future programming designers; it is a significant expertise for people across different fields. Coding encourages computational reasoning, critical thinking, and inventiveness. Incorporating coding into the educational plan outfits understudies with the abilities expected to draw in with arising advances, like man-made intelligence and computerization, and engages them to contribute genuinely to a carefully determined world. Besides, coding schooling supports an outlook of nonstop learning and versatility, planning understudies for the powerful idea of the gig market.

Decisive reasoning and critical thinking abilities are immortal capabilities that gain recharged importance with regards to a robotized future. As normal undertakings become computerized, the labor force is progressively entrusted with taking care of intricate issues and pursuing key choices. Training should develop decisive reasoning abilities that include examining data, assessing choices, and making good decisions. Critical thinking, a necessary part of decisive reasoning, remains closely connected with versatility, imagination, and strength - characteristics that are essential in exploring the vulnerabilities of a computerized world.

Inventiveness is arising as a remarkably human expertise that supplements the capacities of robotization. While machines succeed at routine and rule-based undertakings, inventiveness stays a human quality that drives development. Schooling should focus on the improvement of inventive reasoning, empowering understudies to investigate, question, and create original thoughts. Inventive critical thinking, creative articulation, and configuration believing are basic parts of an educational plan that looks to cultivate the innovative limits of people.

Supporting imagination not just plans understudies for jobs in imaginative ventures yet additionally imparts an outlook that is versatile and open to development in different expert spaces.

Interdisciplinary learning is acquiring unmistakable quality as an all encompassing way to deal with training in the computerized period. The interconnected idea of current difficulties frequently requires arrangements that draw from various disciplines. Instructive organizations ought to separate storehouses and work with coordinated effort between different fields, empowering understudies to investigate associations among subjects and apply information in an all encompassing way. Interdisciplinary training plans people for the intricacies of certifiable critical thinking, where different viewpoints and aptitude are fundamental.

Delicate abilities, including correspondence, cooperation, and the capacity to appreciate people on a deeper level, are necessary to outcome in a computerized future. As working environments become more powerful and cooperative, the capacity to work successfully in groups, impart thoughts obviously, and explore relational connections becomes vital. Training should put an elevated accentuation on the improvement of these delicate abilities, setting out open doors for understudies to take part in bunch tasks, introductions, and experiential discovering that reflect certifiable expert situations. Also, cultivating the capacity to appreciate anyone on a deeper level, the capacity to comprehend and deal with one's feelings and relate to other people, adds to viable administration and coordinated effort in the mechanized work environment.

Deep rooted learning is presently not a decision yet a need despite fast mechanical progressions. School systems should embrace the idea of deep rooted picking up, imparting in understudies the worth of constant personal development and variation. This includes making a culture where learning isn't restricted to formal instructive foundations however reaches out into the work environment and then some. The reconciliation of internet learning stages, miniature credentialing, and adaptable learning models permits people to procure new abilities at their own speed, cultivating a mentality of unending development and improvement.

Experiential getting the hang of, including temporary jobs, apprenticeships, and genuine tasks, is a foundation of planning understudies for the requests of a robotized future. Hypothetical information alone is deficient; pragmatic application and involved encounters give a scaffold between the study hall and the working environment. Instructive establishments ought to produce organizations with enterprises, offering understudies chances to apply their abilities in bona fide settings. Experiential learning upgrades specialized capability as well as fosters the critical thinking, correspondence, and collaboration abilities vital for outcome in the expert field.

The job of teachers is significant during the time spent reconsidering instruction for a robotized future. Educators should advance into facilitators of getting the hang of, directing understudies in creating decisive reasoning abilities, encouraging imagination, and imparting an enthusiasm

for deep rooted learning. Proficient improvement open doors for instructors ought to zero in on keeping up to date with mechanical progressions, consolidating creative educational methodologies, and adjusting to the changing requirements of understudies and the work market. Moreover, cultivating a development mentality among teachers adds to a culture of persistent improvement and flexibility notwithstanding instructive changes.

Inclusivity and variety should be basic parts of rethought school systems. As the labor force turns out to be more different, training should reflect and commend this variety. Comprehensive educational plans that address different points of view, societies, and encounters add to a more extravagant learning climate. Also, making pathways for underrepresented gatherings to get to quality schooling and partake in STEM (science, innovation, designing, and math) fields is fundamental for guaranteeing an impartial conveyance of chances in the mechanized future.

Instructive organizations ought to use arising advancements to upgrade opportunities for growth. Virtual and increased reality, man-made intelligence fueled instructive apparatuses, and online stages can work with customized picking up, permitting understudies to advance at their own speed and investigate areas of premium. Gamification and re-production based learning conditions give vivid encounters that draw in understudies and foster pragmatic abilities. The joining of innovation in training not just gets ready understudies for a tech-driven work environment yet in addition upgrades the viability of educating systems.

Strategy systems assume a critical part in supporting the change of schooling for a robotized future. Policymakers should team up with teachers, industry pioneers, and different partners to foster methodologies that adjust schooling to the advancing necessities of the gig market. This includes reconsidering state administered testing, advancing adaptability in educational plan, and boosting instructive establishments to embrace imaginative methodologies. Strategies that focus on interest in STEM schooling, educator preparing, and drives to address instructive disparities add to building a versatile and versatile labor force.

Public-private organizations are instrumental in overcoming any barrier among training and industry. Coordinated effort between instructive foundations and organizations guarantees that educational programs are applicable to the abilities requested by the gig market.

Industry input in the plan of instructive projects, arrangement of temporary jobs, and cooperation in mentorship drives makes a consistent change from schooling to business. Besides, organizations can add to the continuous expert improvement of the labor force, cultivating a culture of ceaseless advancing inside their associations.

2.4 Ensuring Inclusive Opportunities in the Automated Workforce

Guaranteeing comprehensive open doors in the robotized labor force is a basic as social orders wrestle with the extraordinary effect of robotization, computerized reasoning (man-made intelligence), and cutting edge innovations. The developing idea of work requests a deliberate work to address expected inconsistencies and guarantee that the advantages of innovative headways are impartially conveyed across different populaces.

This includes admittance to business open doors as well as the improvement of abilities, the making of comprehensive working environment societies, and the thought of cultural designs that might propagate imbalance.

A foundation of guaranteeing comprehensive open doors in the mechanized labor force is tending to the computerized partition. Variations in admittance to innovation and advanced framework can fuel existing disparities, restricting specific populaces' capacity to partake completely in the computerized economy. Endeavors should be made to connect this gap by giving reasonable and open innovation, guaranteeing dependable web network, and offering computerized proficiency programs. This is especially pivotal for minimized networks, country populaces, and people with restricted admittance to instructive assets.

Ability improvement and schooling assume vital parts in encouraging inclusivity in the mechanized labor force. Drives pointed toward upskilling and reskilling ought to focus on inclusivity, taking into account the exceptional necessities and conditions of various segment gatherings. Customized preparing programs, grant potential open doors, and mentorship drives can assist with addressing authentic variations in admittance to training and ability improvement. In addition, instructive educational plans ought to be intended to be socially delicate, orientation comprehensive, and receptive to different learning styles, guaranteeing that all people can flourish in the robotized time.

Orientation value is a critical part of guaranteeing comprehensive open doors in the robotized labor force. By and large, certain businesses and jobs have been vigorously orientation slanted, and there is a gamble that robotization might propagate or fuel these orientation variations. Endeavors ought to be coordinated towards separating orientation generalizations, empowering young ladies and ladies to seek after STEM (science, innovation, designing, and arithmetic) fields, and advancing equivalent open doors in customarily male-overwhelmed areas. Also, tending to predisposition in simulated intelligence calculations and innovation configuration is fundamental to forestall the propagation of orientation based imbalances in robotized frameworks.

People with handicaps should be effectively remembered for the talk on comprehensive open doors in the computerized labor force. Innovation can possibly upgrade openness and make additional opportunities for people with incapacities. Notwithstanding, it is critical to guarantee that the plan of computerized frameworks and working environments considers different capacities. This includes making computerized stages, applications, and connection points open, as well as encouraging work environment conditions that oblige the requirements of people with incapacities. Comprehensive recruiting rehearses that consider the qualities and capacities of people with incapacities add to a labor force that mirrors the variety of society.

The multifacetedness of characters should be recognized in the mission for comprehensive open doors. People might confront numerous layers of separation in view of variables like race, orientation, financial status, and sexual direction. Comprehensive approaches and drives ought to perceive and address these converging personalities, guaranteeing that nobody is abandoned in the change to a mechanized labor force. Besides, cultivating a working environment culture that values variety and incorporation requires a thorough methodology that thinks about the special encounters and viewpoints of people with meeting personalities.

Local area commitment and associations are instrumental in advancing comprehensive open doors in the robotized labor force. Coordinated efforts between government organizations, non-benefit associations, instructive establishments, and organizations can make comprehensive arrangements that address the diverse difficulties of inclusivity. Local area based drives, for example, mentorship programs, work fairs, and abilities improvement studios, can assume a pivotal part in arriving at different populaces and guaranteeing that the advantages of mechanization are circulated evenhandedly.

Strategy structures assume a focal part in forming comprehensive open doors in the robotized labor force. States should sanction strategies that elevate equivalent admittance to instruction, preparing, and business open doors. This incorporates hostile to segregation regulations, governmental policy regarding minorities in society measures, and motivations for organizations to embrace comprehensive practices. Moreover, approaches ought to address the moral contemplations encompassing robotization, like the potential for algorithmic predisposition and the effect of computerization on unambiguous segment gatherings. Standard checking and appraisal of the effect of arrangements on inclusivity are fundamental for refining methodologies and guaranteeing supported progress.

Comprehensive open doors in the mechanized labor force likewise require a change in hierarchical practices and corporate culture. Organizations should focus on variety, value, and incorporation (DEI) drives as fundamental parts of their techniques. This includes executing comprehensive recruiting works on, giving equivalent open doors to proficient turn of events, and encouraging working environment conditions that esteem assorted points of view. Straightforward covering variety measurements, pay value, and portrayal at all levels of the association is fundamental for responsibility and ceaseless improvement.

Advancing business among underrepresented bunches is a strong methodology for guaranteeing comprehensive open doors. Business venture gives people the organization to set out their own open doors and add to financial development. Drives that help minority-possessed organizations, ladies business visionaries, and people from underestimated networks can groundbreakingly affect comprehensive financial turn of events. Admittance to financing, mentorship projects, and organizations that interface business visionaries with assets are critical parts of encouraging a different and comprehensive innovative biological system.

Moral contemplations in the plan and organization of mechanized frameworks are principal to guaranteeing inclusivity. The potential for algorithmic inclination, prejudicial results, and unseen side-effects of computerization should be thoroughly tended to. Moral rules and guidelines ought to be laid out to oversee the turn of events and utilization of mechanized innovations, with an emphasis on straightforwardness, responsibility, and reasonableness. Connecting with assorted partners, including agents from minimized networks, in the moral talk encompassing robotization is fundamental to abstain from supporting existing disparities.

Worldwide coordinated effort is fundamental in tending to the difficulties of comprehensive open doors in the robotized labor force. As computerization rises above public limits, deliberate endeavors on a global scale are essential. Sharing prescribed procedures, trading experiences, and teaming up on exploration can add to the advancement of comprehensive arrangements and systems that are versatile to different social settings. Worldwide associations between state run administrations, organizations, and common society associations can enhance the effect of drives pointed toward encouraging inclusivity in the computerized labor force.

Public mindfulness and training are key parts of guaranteeing comprehensive open doors in the mechanized labor force. Educating the general population about the ramifications regarding mechanization, the potential for inclination, and the significance of inclusivity can enable people to advocate for evenhanded arrangements and practices. Training efforts that feature examples of overcoming adversity of people from underrepresented bunches in the tech and robotization fields can rouse the future and challenge generalizations. Besides, encouraging a culture of consistent gaining and versatility guarantees that people from all foundations can flourish in the developing scene of work.

The idea of comprehensive open doors in the robotized labor force stretches out past addressing prompt difficulties to envelop the more extensive reconsidering of cultural designs and standards. Accomplishing genuine inclusivity requires a diverse methodology that thinks about verifiable imbalances, fundamental inclinations, and the developing elements of the labor force. As social orders explore the intricacies of the computerized period, a few key aspects arise that add to an extensive comprehension of comprehensive open doors.

Authentic Setting and Disparities:

To really address inclusivity in the mechanized labor force, critical to recognize authentic imbalances have molded admittance to training, work, and financial open doors. Networks that have generally been minimized or oppressed may confront intensified difficulties in the time of computerization. For instance, tending to variations in instructive results among various segment bunches is fundamental for making an underpinning of equivalent open door. Perceiving the verifiable setting takes into consideration designated mediations that destroy obstructions and advance a more level battleground.

Impartial Admittance to Training:

Schooling fills in as the foundation of inclusivity in the mechanized labor force. Endeavors to guarantee equivalent admittance to quality schooling should stretch out from essential levels to advanced education and professional preparation. Financial elements, geographic area, and social contemplations can impact instructive open doors. Drives, for example, grant programs, local area based learning places, and mentorship plans can assume a urgent part in evening out the instructive battleground. Additionally, educational plans ought to be planned with social awareness and significance to different populaces, cultivating a climate where all understudies feel seen and esteemed.

Social Ability and Coaching in racial awareness:

Chasing after comprehensive open doors, associations should focus on social capability and racial awareness coaching. This includes developing a comprehension of assorted viewpoints, foundations, and encounters inside the labor force. Preparing projects ought to advance sympathy, relational abilities, and an appreciation for the lavishness that variety brings to the working environment. Building comprehensive hierarchical societies requires a promise to value at all levels, from enlistment and recruiting practices to advancement and initiative turn of events. A different labor force reflects cultural socioeconomics as well as upgrades innovativeness, development, and critical thinking capacities.

Tending to Predisposition in Robotized Frameworks:

The potential for predisposition in robotized frameworks represents a critical test to inclusivity. AI calculations, whenever prepared on one-sided datasets, can propagate and try and intensify existing imbalances. Guaranteeing that computerized frameworks are fair and unprejudiced requires continuous investigation, straightforwardness, and responsibility. The turn of events and arrangement of calculations should include different groups to relieve the gamble of unexpected inclination. Also, consistent observing and assessment of robotized frameworks can recognize and redress predispositions as they arise.

Diversity in Comprehensive Techniques:

A comprehensive methodology should perceive and represent diversity — the interconnected idea of social orders like race, orientation, financial status, and that's just the beginning. Diversity underlines that people experience separation in changing ways relying upon the convergence of their characters. Comprehensive techniques ought to, subsequently, consider the exceptional difficulties looked by those with meeting characters. For example, a lady of variety might experience unexpected hindrances in comparison to a white lady or a man of variety.

Perceiving and tending to these convergences is significant for making arrangements and drives that really benefit all people.

Comprehensive Business venture and Financial Strengthening:

Advancing business venture among underrepresented bunches is a useful asset for guaranteeing financial strengthening and inclusivity. Drives that offer monetary help, mentorship, and systems administration valuable open doors to minority-possessed organizations add to a more comprehensive financial scene. Legislatures and confidential area associations can assume a critical part in making environments that help different business people. Furthermore, admittance to capital, business training, and market open doors are fundamental parts of cultivating comprehensive business.

Adaptable Work Game plans and Openness:

The development of work in the robotized time ought to embrace adaptable game plans that oblige different necessities. Remote work, adaptable hours, and other elective work designs can help people with changing capacities, family obligations, or wellbeing contemplations. Businesses ought to focus on establishing conditions that help balance between serious and fun activities and think about the openness of work environments for people with handicaps. Embracing adaptability improves inclusivity as well as adds to expanded efficiency and occupation fulfillment.

Worldwide Cooperation for Inclusivity:

In the interconnected universe of computerization, worldwide joint effort is basic for guaranteeing comprehensive open doors. Information sharing, prescribed procedures, and cooperative examination endeavors can add to a more nuanced comprehension of inclusivity difficulties and arrangements. Global organizations can work with the trading of thoughts, assets, and methodologies for establishing comprehensive workplaces. Moreover, resolving worldwide issues, for example, the computerized partition requires purposeful endeavors on a worldwide scale, recognizing that inclusivity isn't restricted by public lines.

Strategy Promotion and Legitimate Systems:

The turn of events and authorization of strong lawful structures are crucial to advancing inclusivity. States assume a vital part in upholding for strategies that safeguard against separation, guarantee equivalent open doors, and consider associations responsible for comprehensive practices. Against separation regulations, equivalent compensation regulation, and measures to address work environment provocation are fundamental parts of encouraging comprehensive open doors. Support from common society associations and people can add to forming strategies that mirror the upsides of inclusivity and value.

Emotional wellness and Prosperity:

Inclusivity stretches out past unmistakable chances to envelop emotional well-being and prosperity. The working environment, frequently a critical part of people's lives, ought to focus on establishing conditions that help emotional wellness.

This includes destigmatizing psychological wellness issues, giving admittance to guiding administrations, and cultivating a culture of compassion and backing. Comprehensive open doors shouldn't come at the expense of people's prosperity however ought to add to an all encompassing feeling of satisfaction and fulfillment in both individual and expert circles.

The Job of Innovation in Inclusivity:

While innovation can here and there be a wellspring of imbalance, it likewise holds huge potential for encouraging inclusivity. Assistive advances, for instance, can engage people with inabilities by giving devices to correspondence, versatility, and admittance to data. Besides, innovation can work with remote work, online training, and virtual cooperation, separating topographical boundaries and growing open doors for assorted populaces. A cognizant work to outfit innovation for inclusivity requires progressing examination, development, and joint effort between the tech business and associations zeroed in on friendly effect.

Local area Strengthening and Grassroots Drives:

Nearby people group assume an essential part in advancing inclusivity. Grassroots drives that enable local area individuals, address explicit necessities, and make encouraging groups of people add to a more comprehensive society. Local area based associations, non-benefits, and support gatherings can act as impetuses for change by understanding the special difficulties looked by their constituents and pushing for arrangements that reflect local area needs. Drawing in networks in the discussion about inclusivity guarantees that arrangements are logically applicable and successful.

Comprehensive Promoting and Media Portrayal:

The media and promoting businesses use huge impact in molding cultural discernments. Inclusivity in promoting, media portrayal, and narrating can challenge generalizations and add to a more fair culture. Brands and news sources that effectively embrace variety in their informing mirror the truth of different social orders as well as add to forming view of what is viewed as typical, satisfactory, and optimistic.

Persistent Assessment and Transformation:

Inclusivity is certainly not a static objective however a continuous interaction that requires nonstop assessment and transformation. Standard appraisals of arrangements, practices, and results are fundamental for recognizing regions that need improvement. Criticism from workers, partners, and networks can give important bits of knowledge into the viability of inclusivity drives. Associations focused on inclusivity ought to be spry and responsive, putting forth essential acclimations to guarantee that their attempts line up with advancing cultural requirements.

Chapter 3

Human-AI Collaboration in the Workplace

Human-man-made intelligence joint effort in the work environment addresses a change in outlook that can possibly rethink how undertakings are achieved, choices are made, and development is encouraged. As man-made brainpower (simulated intelligence) keeps on propelling, the reconciliation of artificial intelligence frameworks close by human specialists has turned into a critical element of the cutting edge workplace. This coordinated effort, portrayed by the reciprocal qualities of people and man-made intelligence, holds commitments of expanded effectiveness, upgraded critical thinking capacities, and the production of new open doors. Be that as it may, it likewise presents difficulties connected with work relocation, moral contemplations, and the requirement for a reexamination of customary work structures.

One of the central parts of human-computer based intelligence joint effort is the cooperative energy between human innovativeness and the computational force of artificial intelligence. While man-made intelligence succeeds in handling immense measures of information and executing dreary errands with accuracy, people bring imagination, instinct, and the ability to appreciate anyone on a deeper level to the table.

This integral relationship opens roads for development and critical thinking that influence the qualities of the two players. For example, in imaginative businesses, artificial intelligence devices can aid information examination and example acknowledgment, opening up human creatives to zero in on ideation and the more nuanced parts of their work.

Cooperative robots, or cobots, address an unmistakable sign of human-simulated intelligence joint effort on the industrial facility floor. These robots work close by human laborers, performing undertakings that require accuracy and strength, while people handle more intricate and mental parts of the work. The outcome is a more effective and smoothed out creation process. This cooperative methodology upgrades efficiency, further develops wellbeing via mechanizing perilous assignments, and permits human specialists to zero in on errands that require critical thinking, decisive reasoning, and versatility.

In any case, the joining of computer based intelligence in the working environment raises worries about work removal and the changing idea of work. As specific routine errands become robotized, there is a genuine feeling of dread toward employment cutback in specific ventures. This requires a proactive way to deal with labor force improvement, with an emphasis on upskilling and reskilling to adjust the labor force to the developing requests of the gig market. It is urgent to see simulated intelligence as a device that expands human capacities as opposed to a substitution, encouraging an outlook of cooperation and flexibility.

Moral contemplations pose a potential threat in the scene of human-simulated intelligence coordinated effort. Issues, for example, algorithmic inclination, protection concerns, and the moral treatment of computer based intelligence frameworks request cautious consideration. Predispositions implanted in artificial intelligence calculations, frequently intelligent of verifiable human inclinations present in preparing information, can sustain and try and compound existing disparities. Finding some kind of harmony between the advantages of computer based intelligence and moral contemplations requires continuous examination, straightforwardness, and the improvement of moral rules that focus on reasonableness and responsibility.

As man-made intelligence frameworks become fundamental to dynamic cycles, straightforwardness is pivotal for building trust in human-artificial intelligence cooperation. Understanding how computer based intelligence shows up at choices, the elements it considers, and the potential predispositions it might hold onto is fundamental for guaranteeing responsibility. This straightforwardness isn't just a question of moral obligation yet additionally a down to earth need for organizations and associations to construct and keep up with entrust with workers and partners.

The changing elements of the working environment require a reconsideration of customary schooling and preparing models. The abilities expected for successful human-computer based intelligence cooperation stretch out past specialized capability to incorporate decisive reasoning, versatility, and the capacity to appreciate anyone on a deeper level.

Instructive foundations should adjust their educational programs to furnish understudies with the abilities expected to explore an undeniably mechanized world. Long lasting learning drives, constant preparation, and improvement programs become fundamental parts of a labor force that is ready for the difficulties and open doors introduced by human-simulated intelligence cooperation.

The idea of expanded knowledge, where artificial intelligence frameworks increase human decision-production instead of supplant it, is vital to the way of thinking of human-computer based intelligence cooperation. Expanded knowledge recognizes that while man-made intelligence can deal with tremendous measures of information and distinguish designs, it comes up short on nuanced grasping, instinct, and context oriented mindfulness intrinsic in human discernment. In cooperative dynamic cycles, man-made intelligence frameworks can give information driven experiences, liberating human leaders to zero in on essential reasoning and the moral contemplations intrinsic in complex decisions.

Human-artificial intelligence coordinated effort isn't bound to routine undertakings; it stretches out to innovative and mental undertakings. In fields, for example, medical care, simulated intelligence is utilized to break down clinical pictures, recognize examples, and aid diagnostics. Human specialists work close by simulated intelligence frameworks, utilizing the productivity of innovation while holding the decisive reasoning and sympathy expected for patient consideration. This cooperative model upgrades the exactness and speed of diagnostics, at last working on quiet results.

In client support, chatbots and menial helpers controlled by artificial intelligence handle routine questions and errands, permitting human client assistance agents to participate in more mind boggling and genuinely nuanced cooperations. This upgrades the productivity of client care as well as adds to a really fulfilling client experience. Human-manmade intelligence joint effort in this setting is intended to profit by the qualities of each, making a cooperative energy that benefits the two organizations and clients.

Notwithstanding, the mix of computer based intelligence in client support likewise raises moral contemplations, especially with respect to straightforwardness and the divulgence of man-made intelligence association. Clients reserve an option to know whether they are collaborating with a human or a man-made intelligence framework, and organizations should focus on clear correspondence to construct trust. Finding some kind of harmony among computerization and human touch is fundamental to making a positive client experience.

The idea of reasonable simulated intelligence is acquiring unmistakable quality as associations perceive the significance of understanding how artificial intelligence shows up at explicit choices. In settings like medical services or money, where choices have critical outcomes, the capacity to make sense of the reasoning behind artificial intelligence driven choices is significant.

Logical artificial intelligence improves straightforwardness as well as encourages trust and responsibility, addressing concerns connected with one-sided calculations and unseen side-effects.

Cooperation between human originators and simulated intelligence frameworks is molding the eventual fate of imaginative undertakings. In fields like visual communication, music organization, and content creation, simulated intelligence apparatuses are helping human makers in creating thoughts, investigating prospects, and in any event, delivering content. This cooperative methodology doesn't supplant human innovativeness however increases it, offering new instruments and viewpoints that push the limits of what is conceivable. The outcome is a unique exchange between human inventiveness and machine-produced yields, prompting novel and imaginative results.

The execution of simulated intelligence in the recruiting system is one more feature of human-simulated intelligence coordinated effort. Simulated intelligence instruments can smooth out the underlying phases of enrollment by investigating resumes, recognizing likely applicants, and in any event, leading fundamental meetings. Notwithstanding, this raises worries about algorithmic predisposition and the possible support of existing abberations in employing. Human oversight and mediation are fundamental to guarantee reasonableness, alleviate predispositions, and maintain moral guidelines in the recruiting system.

The mental effect of man-made intelligence in the work environment is an area of progressing exploration and thought. The apprehension about work relocation, worries about reconnaissance, and the potential for man-made intelligence to add to a more distressing workplace all request cautious consideration. Associations should focus on worker prosperity and emotional well-being, giving assets and emotionally supportive networks to address the mental ramifications of artificial intelligence combination. Straightforward correspondence about the job of simulated intelligence, its restrictions, and the goals behind its execution can add to a positive hierarchical culture.

Joint effort among people and artificial intelligence additionally stretches out to the domain of prescient investigation for business technique. Simulated intelligence frameworks can break down market patterns, customer conduct, and serious scenes, giving important bits of knowledge that illuminate key direction. Human pioneers, outfitted with these experiences, can then figure out methodologies, settle on informed decisions, and adjust to dynamic economic situations. This cooperative methodology improves hierarchical deftness and responsiveness.

Security worries in the time of human-simulated intelligence cooperation require powerful information assurance measures. As man-made intelligence frameworks process immense measures of individual and delicate information, guaranteeing the protection and security of this data is foremost.

Consistence with information insurance guidelines, straightforward information rehearses, and the execution of encryption and secure stockpiling measures are fundamental parts of moral computer based intelligence sending. Associations should focus on the turn of events and adherence to security arrangements that shield the freedoms and interests of people.

The job of administration and guidelines in regulating human-man-made intelligence cooperation is a basic thought. As simulated intelligence turns out to be progressively coordinated into different parts of society, administrative structures should keep speed to guarantee capable and moral use. States, industry bodies, and global associations assume an essential part in creating and implementing guidelines that oversee the organization of artificial intelligence. This incorporates contemplations of responsibility, straightforwardness, and the moral treatment of man-made intelligence frameworks.

3.1 Augmented Intelligence: A Human-AI Synergy

Increased insight, frequently named as the cooperative joint effort among people and computerized reasoning (man-made intelligence), addresses a groundbreaking worldview that saddles the qualities of the two elements to accomplish synergistic results. Dissimilar to the idea of artificial intelligence as a substitution for human capacities, expanded insight stresses the upgrade of human navigation and critical thinking through the mix of trend setting innovations. This approach recognizes that while simulated intelligence frameworks succeed in handling and breaking down immense datasets, people contribute one of a kind characteristics like instinct, imagination, and moral thinking. The convergence of human resourcefulness with the computational force of computer based intelligence holds the commitment of tending to complex difficulties, cultivating development, and molding a future where innovation is an instrument for human strengthening.

At its center, expanded knowledge looks to conquer the limits of the two people and artificial intelligence while working in detachment. Human comprehension has innate predispositions, is inclined to weariness, and may battle with handling monstrous datasets effectively. Then again, computer based intelligence frameworks, while capable at taking care of huge volumes of information and performing monotonous errands, miss the mark on nuanced figuring out, the ability to appreciate individuals on a profound level, and logical mindfulness that people bring to independent direction. Expanded knowledge plans to establish a cooperative climate where every substance makes up for the shortcomings of the other, bringing about a more thorough and powerful critical thinking approach.

One of the vital utilizations of expanded knowledge is in medical services, where the cooperation among people and computer based intelligence is upsetting diagnostics, therapy arranging, and patient consideration. Computer based intelligence calculations, prepared on huge clinical datasets, can help medical services experts in dissecting clinical pictures, distinguishing designs, and anticipating potential medical problems.

This coordinated effort upgrades the precision and speed of determinations, permitting clinical professionals to zero in on customized patient consideration, compassion, and complex navigation. The combination of artificial intelligence in medical care isn't a swap for human mastery yet a device that enhances the capacities of medical care experts, prompting further developed results for patients.

In the domain of business and money, expanded knowledge is reshaping the way that associations break down information, settle on essential choices, and oversee gambles. Computer based intelligence driven examination can process broad monetary datasets, distinguish designs, and give experiences that illuminate vital preparation. Human chiefs, equipped with these information driven bits of knowledge, can then apply their essential reasoning, industry mastery, and moral contemplations to settle on informed choices. This cooperative methodology upgrades hierarchical spryness, further develops risk the board, and takes into account more compelling reactions to dynamic economic situations.

The idea of increased insight additionally reaches out to client support, where artificial intelligence fueled chatbots and remote helpers team up with human agents to improve the general client experience. Chatbots can deal with routine questions, give moment reactions, and help with fundamental critical thinking, opening up human specialists to zero in on more perplexing and sincerely nuanced cooperations. This coordinated effort smoothes out client support tasks, increments proficiency, and adds to a really fulfilling client experience. The key is to find some kind of harmony among computerization and the human touch, guaranteeing that clients feel appreciated, comprehended, and esteemed.

In the field of schooling, expanded knowledge is being utilized to customize opportunities for growth, adjust to individual understudy needs, and give continuous criticism. Artificial intelligence calculations dissect understudy execution information, recognize learning designs, and suggest customized learning ways. Teachers, in a joint effort with artificial intelligence frameworks, can then tailor their showing draws near, address explicit learning holes, and make a seriously captivating and powerful learning climate. This cooperative model perceives the variety of learning styles and streamlines the instructive experience for every understudy.

Notwithstanding the bunch advantages of expanded knowledge, moral contemplations are principal in its execution. Issues, for example, algorithmic inclination, security concerns, and the moral treatment of simulated intelligence frameworks require cautious consideration. The predispositions present in preparing information can be sustained by artificial intelligence calculations, prompting oppressive results. Straightforwardness in how artificial intelligence shows up at choices, responsibility for the results of computerized processes, and a promise to reasonableness are fundamental parts of moral expanded knowledge.

Finding some kind of harmony between the benefits of man-made intelligence and moral contemplations requests continuous investigation and the advancement of rules that focus on inclusivity and responsibility.

The medical care area gives a convincing delineation of how increased knowledge tends to moral contemplations. Artificial intelligence calculations utilized for diagnostics and treatment suggestions should go through thorough testing to guarantee exactness, dependability, and decency across assorted patient populaces. Straightforward correspondence about the capacities and limits of computer based intelligence frameworks is vital for building trust between medical care experts, patients, and the innovation. The moral utilization of expanded knowledge in medical care includes a ceaseless exchange, informed assent, and a promise to focusing on quiet prosperity.

With regards to enlistment and recruiting, increased knowledge is utilized to smooth out processes, break down resumes, and recognize expected applicants. Be that as it may, moral worries emerge with respect to algorithmic predisposition and the support of existing abberations in recruiting. Human oversight and mediation are important to guarantee reasonableness, moderate inclinations, and maintain moral guidelines. Straightforwardness in the utilization of computer based intelligence in recruiting rehearses is fundamental for building entrust with work candidates and keeping away from unseen side-effects that might sustain imbalances.

Reasonableness in man-made intelligence, or the capacity to comprehend and decipher how computer based intelligence shows up at explicit choices, is urgent for tending to moral worries. This is especially pertinent in areas like money, medical services, and law enforcement, where computer based intelligence frameworks influence people's lives. The absence of reasonableness can prompt a deficiency of trust and responsibility. Expanded knowledge models that focus on straightforwardness engage human chiefs to comprehend the reasoning behind simulated intelligence driven choices, recognize likely predispositions, and guarantee reasonableness.

The joint effort among people and artificial intelligence in imaginative undertakings acquaints an exceptional aspect with expanded knowledge. Man-made intelligence apparatuses in fields like visual computerization, music arrangement, and content creation can help human makers in producing thoughts, investigating prospects, and in any event, delivering content. This cooperative methodology doesn't supplant human imagination however improves it by offering new apparatuses and viewpoints. The outcome is a unique interchange between human resourcefulness and machine-created yields, prompting novel and imaginative results.

The advancement of moral rules for computer based intelligence in imaginative businesses becomes urgent as the limits among human and machine-produced content haze. Issues of protected innovation, attribution, and the effect of artificial intelligence produced content on conventional imaginative callings require cautious thought. Expanded knowledge in imaginative fields ought to be directed by rules that recognize the commitment of the two people and machines, regard protected innovation freedoms, and encourage a cooperative and moral imaginative environment.

In the work environment, the mental effect of expanded knowledge is an area of continuous exploration and thought. The apprehension about work uprooting, worries about observation, and the potential for simulated intelligence to add to a more unpleasant workplace all request cautious consideration. Associations should focus on worker prosperity and emotional well-being, giving assets and emotionally supportive networks to address the mental ramifications of man-made intelligence combination. Straightforward correspondence about the job of simulated intelligence, its constraints, and the goals behind its execution can add to a positive hierarchical culture.

As artificial intelligence advances keep on developing, the democratization of man-made intelligence instruments and innovations is turning into an arising pattern. The rising openness and ease of use of computer based intelligence stages enable people with fluctuating degrees of specialized aptitude to use these apparatuses for assorted applications. This pattern democratizes development by permitting a more extensive scope of partners, including private companies, business people, and people, to partake in the turn of events and utilization of computer based intelligence. Democratization cultivates imagination, development, and a more comprehensive way to deal with critical thinking.

The changing elements of the work environment require a reconsideration of customary instruction and preparing models. The abilities expected for successful increased insight reach out past specialized capability to incorporate decisive reasoning, flexibility, and the capacity to appreciate individuals on a profound level. Instructive organizations should adjust their educational plans to outfit understudies with the abilities expected to explore an inexorably computerized world. Deep rooted learning drives, consistent preparation, and improvement programs become fundamental parts of a labor force that is ready for the difficulties and valuable open doors introduced by increased knowledge.

Administration and guidelines assume a focal part in directing expanded knowledge. As simulated intelligence becomes necessary to different parts of society, administrative structures should advance to guarantee capable and moral use. States, industry bodies, and worldwide associations play an essential part in creating and upholding guidelines that oversee the organization of simulated intelligence. This incorporates contemplations of responsibility, straightforwardness.

3.2 Designing AI-Enhanced Workspaces

Planning artificial intelligence upgraded work areas addresses a significant wilderness in the development of the cutting edge working environment, where the mix of man-made reasoning (computer based intelligence) advancements expects to improve proficiency, encourage development, and improve the general work insight. As associations progressively perceive the capability of man-made intelligence to increase human abilities, the plan of work areas is advancing to consistently oblige these innovations. From savvy robotization to customized encounters, the combination of artificial intelligence in work area configuration holds the commitment of changing how work is directed, establishing conditions that adjust to the requirements of people and groups while encouraging cooperation and efficiency.

At the center of planning computer based intelligence improved work areas is the acknowledgment that computer based intelligence isn't an independent instrument yet an indispensable piece of the general work environment. Savvy computerization, driven by artificial intelligence, is reshaping standard and dreary undertakings, permitting human laborers to zero in on more mind boggling, imaginative, and vital parts of their jobs. In this unique circumstance, work area configuration should work with the consistent combination of man-made intelligence advancements into day to day work processes, guaranteeing that mechanization improves, as opposed to upsets, human efficiency.

One of the critical contemplations in artificial intelligence upgraded work area configuration is the execution of brilliant foundation and IoT (Web of Things) gadgets. These innovations empower the assortment of constant information on work area use, natural circumstances, and representative exercises. Artificial intelligence calculations can then dissect this information to improve factors like lighting, temperature, and guest plans in view of individual inclinations and work designs. This degree of personalization adds to a more agreeable and useful workplace, where the work area adjusts to the necessities of every representative.

Coordinated effort is a foundation of current work, and simulated intelligence upgraded work areas assume a vital part in working with consistent cooperation among colleagues, paying little mind to actual area. Artificial intelligence driven joint effort instruments, like virtual gathering aides and canny undertaking the board frameworks, upgrade correspondence, smooth out work processes, and give experiences into group elements. The plan of cooperative spaces, both physical and virtual, should represent the incorporation of these instruments to help powerful collaboration and cultivate a culture of development.

The idea of expanded reality (AR) and augmented reality (VR) is acquiring unmistakable quality in computer based intelligence improved work area plan. AR overlays advanced data onto the actual climate, improving certifiable encounters, while VR makes vivid, PC created conditions.

These advancements have applications in preparing, plan, and distant coordinated effort. In the plan of work areas, contemplations incorporate making committed regions for AR/VR exercises, guaranteeing similarity with existing advances, and giving ergonomic answers for expanded use.

Customized UIs driven by computer based intelligence are reshaping the way that people interface with their workplaces. From savvy collaborators that learn client inclinations to versatile connection points that expect client needs, simulated intelligence adds to a more instinctive and client driven work area plan. The test lies in offsetting personalization with protection concerns and guaranteeing that simulated intelligence driven interfaces improve, as opposed to overpower, the client experience. Planning work areas that offer adaptable man-made intelligence highlights engages people to fit their surroundings to suit their functioning styles.

The mix of computer based intelligence in work area configuration additionally stretches out to the idea of wise furnishings and gear. Savvy work areas that change level in view of client inclinations, seats that give ergonomic criticism, and man-made intelligence driven lighting frameworks that adjust to circadian rhythms are instances of how actual work areas can be upgraded through innovation. Planning computer based intelligence upgraded furniture requires joint effort between furniture originators and computer based intelligence specialists to make consistent and easy to understand arrangements that improve both solace and efficiency.

Simulated intelligence driven examination assume a urgent part in work area streamlining. By investigating information on representative way of behaving, space usage, and natural elements, associations can arrive at informed conclusions about work area plan and asset allotment. Planning work areas that oblige sensors and information assortment gadgets without compromising security requires cautious thought of information administration, moral use, and straightforward correspondence with representatives. The objective is to use investigation for the aggregate advantage of the association and its labor force.

The job of artificial intelligence in upgrading worker prosperity is a huge part of work area plan. Artificial intelligence controlled wellbeing applications can screen factors, for example, feelings of anxiety, actual work, and rest designs, giving bits of knowledge that add to representative wellbeing and efficiency. Planning work areas that incorporate these health innovations includes making committed regions for prosperity exercises, guaranteeing information security and protection, and encouraging a culture that values representative wellbeing.

The shift towards remote and adaptable work game plans is another pattern affecting simulated intelligence upgraded work area plan. Manmade intelligence advancements that help virtual cooperation, robotize routine errands, and give customized encounters add to the adequacy of remote work arrangements.

Planning work areas that take special care of both face to face and distant joint effort includes making cross breed spaces, executing secure correspondence advances, and guaranteeing that telecommuters approach a similar man-made intelligence driven devices as their in-office partners.

Integrating computer based intelligence into the actual plan of office spaces requires an insightful way to deal with establish conditions that encourage inventiveness, coordinated effort, and worker prosperity. The format of work areas, the selection of materials, and the incorporation of innovation mixed components all add to the general plan. For example, the position of cooperative regions, the reconciliation of green spaces, and the consolidation of computer based intelligence driven craftsmanship establishments add to an all encompassing and rousing workplace.

Moral contemplations are foremost in artificial intelligence improved work area configuration, especially concerning representative protection, information security, and the capable utilization of artificial intelligence advancements. Straightforward correspondence about the sending of simulated intelligence, clear arrangements on information assortment and use, and hearty safety efforts are fundamental parts of moral work area plan. The objective is to guarantee that the combination of computer based intelligence lines up with moral guidelines and regards the privileges and protection of people inside the work area.

The execution of computer based intelligence upgraded work areas requires a key and cooperative methodology including different partners, including planners, inside originators, IT experts, and HR groups. Cross-disciplinary coordinated effort guarantees that man-made intelligence advances are flawlessly incorporated into the general plan, lining up with authoritative objectives and the requirements of representatives. Planning work areas that focus on coordinated effort between various expert spaces is urgent for the fruitful execution of simulated intelligence driven arrangements.

Ceaseless transformation and adaptability are key standards in the plan of simulated intelligence upgraded work areas. As innovation develops and hierarchical necessities change, work areas should be intended to oblige new simulated intelligence advancements and adjust to moving work elements. Establishing measured and adaptable workplaces guarantees that associations can use the most recent progressions in man-made intelligence without the requirement for broad upgrades. The objective is to future-verification work areas, permitting them to advance close by the developing scene of computer based intelligence.

Worker commitment is a focal thought in simulated intelligence upgraded work area plan. Computer based intelligence innovations that improve correspondence, smooth out work processes, and give customized encounters add to a positive representative encounter.

Planning work areas that focus on representative commitment includes establishing conditions that help both centered work and cooperative exercises. The actual format, decision of furniture, and consolidation of innovation ought to line up determined to encourage a feeling of having a place and fulfillment among workers.

The effect of computer based intelligence upgraded work areas on hierarchical culture is a basic part of plan. Man-made intelligence innovations that advance straightforwardness, cooperation, and inclusivity add to a positive working environment culture. Planning work areas that reflect and support hierarchical qualities includes considering the visual components, the utilization of artificial intelligence driven specialized devices, and the production of spaces that energize social connections. The objective is to adjust the plan of work areas to the ideal social credits of the association.

Schooling and preparing assume a urgent part in guaranteeing that representatives can really explore and use artificial intelligence improved work areas. Planning work areas that help constant learning includes making open preparation programs, giving assets to expertise improvement, and encouraging a culture of interest and flexibility. The objective is to enable workers to take advantage of man-made intelligence innovations and add to the general outcome of the association.

All in all, planning artificial intelligence upgraded work areas addresses a dynamic and multi-layered try that requires an all encompassing methodology. From the actual format of office spaces to the joining of wise advancements, each part of work area configuration assumes a part in molding the eventual fate of work. The effective execution of computer based intelligence upgraded work areas requires coordinated effort, flexibility, and a promise to moral contemplations. As associations embrace the capability of man-made intelligence to expand human capacities, the plan of work areas turns into an essential basic for encouraging development, cooperation, and representative prosperity in the advancing scene of work.

3.3 Nurturing Emotional Intelligence in an Automated Environment

Supporting capacity to understand people on a profound level in a robotized climate is a nuanced and fundamental part of exploring the developing scene of work. As computerization and man-made consciousness (simulated intelligence) keep on reshaping the labor force, the significance of the capacity to appreciate anyone on a profound level — the capacity to perceive, comprehend, and deal with one's own feelings as well as those of others — turns out to be progressively obvious. In this present reality where errands are computerized, the capacity to understand people on a profound level arises as an extraordinarily human expertise that adds to viable correspondence, coordinated effort, and in general prosperity in the working environment.

The combination of computerization and man-made intelligence in the work environment brings up relevant issues about the job of the capacity to understand people on a deeper level in an innovation driven climate. While machines succeed at undertakings that require accuracy, information handling, and effectiveness, they miss the mark on capacity to explore the intricacies of human feelings. The capacity to understand people on a profound level turns into a basic differentiator, empowering people to interface really, construct significant connections, and explore the social subtleties of the work environment.

One of the vital parts of supporting capacity to appreciate people on a profound level is mindfulness — the capacity to perceive and grasp one's own feelings. In a robotized climate, people might wind up communicating with simulated intelligence driven frameworks, teaming up with machines, and overseeing undertakings that include negligible human-to-human collaboration. Mindfulness enables people to figure out their profound reactions to these evolving elements, considering versatility and powerful dynamic in a climate where human-machine coordinated effort is the standard.

Besides, mindfulness assumes a pivotal part in overseeing pressure and staying balanced. The speed of mechanization might prompt expanded jobs or changes in work liabilities. The capacity to understand people on a deeper level outfits people with the mindfulness expected to perceive indications of stress, carry out viable survival strategies, and keep up with mental prosperity. Associations can cultivate mindfulness by advancing care works on, empowering normal self-reflection, and giving assets to push the executives.

One more component of the capacity to understand anyone on a profound level is self-guideline — the capacity to oversee and get a grip on one's own feelings. In a mechanized climate, where errands might be dreary or exceptionally specialized, people need to develop self-guideline to guarantee an amicable workplace. This incorporates the capacity to remain composed under tension, adjust to changes, and manage profound reactions to challenges. Preparing projects and studios zeroed in on pressure the executives, versatility, and flexibility add to the advancement of self-guideline abilities.

The cooperative idea of work in a robotized climate highlights the significance of relational abilities and relationship the board. The ability to understand anyone on a profound level empowers people to explore the intricacies of human connections, fabricate solid connections, and team up successfully with partners, whether human or machine. In group settings, the capacity to comprehend and answer the feelings of others cultivates a good and strong workplace. Associations can energize relational abilities by giving correspondence preparing, advancing group building exercises, and making a culture that values transparent correspondence.

Compassion, a principal part of the capacity to understand people on a deeper level, turns out to be especially critical in a work environment where human-machine coordinated effort is predominant. While machines can handle information proficiently, they miss the mark on capacity to comprehend and relate to the human experience. Supporting sympathy includes encouraging a comprehension of different viewpoints, recognizing the effect of choices on people, and making a working environment culture that values empathy. In group joint efforts, compassion improves correspondence, energizes common help, and adds to a positive and comprehensive workplace.

The convergence of the capacity to understand people on a profound level and initiative is a basic part of overseeing groups in a robotized climate. Pioneers who have the ability to appreciate individuals on a profound level are better prepared to figure out the requirements and worries of their colleagues, rouse inspiration, and explore the close to home scene of the work environment. In a situation where undertakings are robotized, pioneers assume a significant part in developing a culture of the capacity to understand people on a profound level, where colleagues feel upheld, esteemed, and engaged. Authority improvement programs that emphasis on capacity to appreciate people on a profound level add to the making of compelling and sympathetic pioneers.

The moral contemplations inborn in the organization of simulated intelligence and computerization feature the requirement for moral thinking and trustworthiness in the work environment. The ability to understand anyone on a profound level aides people in pursuing moral choices, taking into account the effect of decisions on partners, and exploring circumstances where moral situations might emerge. Associations can sustain moral thinking by incorporating morals preparing into proficient improvement programs, empowering open conversations about moral contemplations, and advancing a qualities driven hierarchical culture.

Flexibility and strength, intently attached to the ability to understand people on a profound level, become fundamental abilities in a mechanized climate portrayed by quick mechanical progressions. People need to explore changes in work jobs, master new abilities, and adjust to advancing work structures. The capacity to understand people at their core adds to flexibility by cultivating a positive mentality, advancing critical thinking abilities, and empowering people to see difficulties as any open doors for development. Associations can uphold versatility by giving nonstop learning open doors, making a culture that values development, and perceiving and commending strength despite change.

The potential for work removal in a computerized climate stresses the significance of the ability to understand people on a deeper level in overseeing vocation changes. People might encounter a scope of feelings, including dread, vulnerability, and disappointment. The capacity to understand people on a profound level prepares people to explore these feelings, look for help, and proactively take part in vocation improvement.

Associations assume a urgent part in supporting representatives through changes by giving profession improvement assets, mentorship programs, and making a culture that esteems the prosperity of its labor force.

The coordination of the capacity to understand individuals on a profound level into simulated intelligence driven connection points and cooperations addresses an interesting element of innovation human joint effort. As simulated intelligence frameworks become more modern, the capacity to perceive and answer human feelings is progressively integrated into UIs and correspondence stages. Planning simulated intelligence interfaces that think about close to home signals, give compassionate reactions, and focus on client prosperity adds to a more easy to use and genuinely savvy innovative scene.

In schooling and preparing, the improvement of the capacity to understand people on a deeper level turns into an essential component in getting ready people for the difficulties of a mechanized future. Instructive foundations and associations should focus on the consideration of the capacity to understand anyone on a deeper level preparation in educational plans and expert improvement programs. This incorporates encouraging close to home mindfulness, relational abilities, and moral thinking from a beginning phase to furnish people with the skills required for outcome in a robotized climate.

The expected effect of man-made intelligence on emotional wellness requires a comprehensive way to deal with prosperity that integrates the capacity to understand individuals on a profound level. People might encounter tension, stress, or sensations of separation because of mechanical changes in the working environment. The ability to appreciate people on a deeper level abilities, like mindfulness and flexibility, are vital in tending to and relieving psychological wellness challenges. Associations can focus on representative prosperity by offering emotional wellness assets, advancing balance between fun and serious activities, and making a strong culture that esteems the comprehensive strength of workers.

The moral plan of computer based intelligence frameworks requires cautious thought of the likely profound effect on clients. Computer based intelligence innovations that connect with people, like remote helpers or chatbots, should be intended to perceive and answer feelings in a mindful and moral way. This includes staying away from circumstances that might inflict any kind of damage, regarding client protection, and focusing on straightforwardness in man-made intelligence cooperations. Moral simulated intelligence configuration lines up with the standards of the capacity to appreciate anyone on a profound level, guaranteeing that innovation regards and improves the close to home prosperity of clients.

The development of the capacity to understand people on a deeper level in a computerized climate reaches out past the person to the hierarchical level. Organizations that focus on capacity to understand people on a deeper level in their way of life and administration add to a

positive and comprehensive working environment. This includes adjusting hierarchical qualities to the capacity to understand individuals on a deeper level standards, encouraging a culture of open correspondence, and perceiving and remunerating ways of behaving that add to a strong workplace. The outcome is an association that esteems the human parts of work close by innovative progressions.

3.4 Ethical Dimensions of AI in Decision-Making

The moral components of man-made consciousness (simulated intelligence) in direction comprise a mind boggling and pivotal part of the continuous talk encompassing the combination of simulated intelligence advances into different features of society. As simulated intelligence frameworks become progressively refined, the choices they make can have significant ramifications for people, associations, and society at large. Investigating the moral contemplations in artificial intelligence direction includes resolving issues like straightforwardness, decency, responsibility, predisposition moderation, and the more extensive cultural effect of computerized choices.

One of the focal moral contemplations in computer based intelligence direction is the straightforwardness of calculations and choice cycles. The haziness of complicated simulated intelligence models can prompt an absence of understanding among end-clients, partners, and, surprisingly, the actual engineers. In circumstances where man-made intelligence frameworks go with choices that influence people's lives, there is an ethical basic for straightforwardness to guarantee responsibility and encourage trust. Moral artificial intelligence configuration focuses on straightforwardness by giving clear clarifications of how calculations show up at explicit choices, empowering clients to grasp the thinking behind mechanized decisions.

The issue of decency in computer based intelligence navigation is intently attached to straightforwardness and is a central moral concern. Computer based intelligence frameworks should be intended to keep away from prejudicial results and treat people genuinely, paying little heed to variables like race, orientation, nationality, or financial status. The presence of predispositions in preparing information can prompt algorithmic inclination, where simulated intelligence frameworks unintentionally propagate or enhance existing cultural imbalances. Moral artificial intelligence professionals endeavor to recognize and alleviate predispositions, guaranteeing that dynamic cycles are fair, evenhanded, and add to civil rights.

Responsibility in man-made intelligence navigation is another basic moral aspect. As man-made intelligence frameworks independently decide, deciding liability in case of mistakes, predispositions, or unseen side-effects becomes testing. Laying out clear lines of responsibility is fundamental for tending to the moral ramifications of robotized choices.

Associations and designers ought to have components set up to follow and comprehend the dynamic interaction, empowering them to assume a sense of ownership with the results of man-made intelligence frameworks. Moral structures underline the requirement for responsibility to forestall the avoidance of obligation in the sending of simulated intelligence advancements.

Relieving predisposition in computer based intelligence navigation is a continuous test that requires devoted consideration from designers, specialists, and associations. Predisposition can appear in different structures, including racial inclination, orientation inclination, and financial inclination, reflecting authentic imbalances present in preparing information. Moral artificial intelligence specialists utilize methods, for example, debiasing calculations, different and delegate information testing, and constant checking to recognize and redress predispositions. Taking a stab at decency and fair-mindedness is basic to the moral sending of man-made intelligence frameworks in dynamic settings.

The moral contemplations of artificial intelligence reach out past individual choices to the more extensive cultural effect of mechanized frameworks. The potential for computer based intelligence to intensify existing social imbalances or make new types of difference highlights the requirement for an exhaustive moral system. Tending to cultural effect includes assessing the drawn out results of artificial intelligence arrangement, taking into account its impacts on business, security, and admittance to assets. Moral dynamic in man-made intelligence requires a comprehensive point of view that thinks about the more extensive ramifications for networks and society all in all.

The idea of reasonableness in computer based intelligence direction is fundamental to tending to moral worries. Reasonableness alludes to the capacity to comprehend and decipher how man-made intelligence frameworks show up at explicit choices. In settings like medical services, money, and law enforcement, where choices have huge results, the capacity to make sense of the reasoning behind man-made intelligence driven choices is significant. Reasonable simulated intelligence improves straightforwardness as well as encourages trust and responsibility, addressing concerns connected with one-sided calculations and potentially negative side-effects.

Security contemplations assume a focal part in the moral elements of computer based intelligence direction, particularly in applications that include individual information. Computer based intelligence frameworks frequently depend on enormous datasets, raising worries about the likely abuse or unapproved admittance to delicate data. Moral artificial intelligence rehearses focus on security by carrying out strong information assurance measures, complying to protection guidelines, and guaranteeing that people have command over their own information. Regarding security freedoms is fundamental for keeping up with trust among clients and man-made intelligence frameworks.

Informed assent is a critical moral guideline in circumstances where simulated intelligence frameworks settle on choices that influence people straightforwardly. Clients ought to be educated about how their information will be utilized, how choices will be made, and what the potential outcomes might be. Giving clear and reasonable data guarantees that people can settle on informed conclusions about whether to draw in with man-made intelligence frameworks. Moral simulated intelligence configuration focuses on informed assent as a basic standard, regarding the independence and freedoms of people.

Guaranteeing the security of computer based intelligence frameworks is a moral objective, especially in dynamic settings where the trustworthiness of calculations and information is central. Artificial intelligence frameworks are helpless against ill-disposed assaults, where pernicious entertainers endeavor to control or take advantage of the dynamic cycle. Moral man-made intelligence experts execute powerful safety efforts, direct weakness appraisals, and focus on the strength of simulated intelligence frameworks against possible dangers. Shielding the security of computer based intelligence innovations is fundamental for forestalling unapproved access, control, or noxious use.

The moral ramifications of occupation removal because of mechanization and computer based intelligence driven independent direction require cautious thought. While computer based intelligence can improve effectiveness and efficiency, it likewise can possibly affect work in specific areas. Moral direction includes a promise to relieving the unfortunate results of occupation relocation, like putting resources into reskilling and upskilling programs, setting out open doors for dislodged laborers to progress to new jobs, and cultivating a cultural exchange on the moral elements of labor force change. Adjusting the advantages of simulated intelligence with social obligation is urgent for moral dynamic in the domain of business.

With regards to law enforcement, the utilization of artificial intelligence in navigation, for example, prescient policing and risk evaluation devices, raises moral worries about predisposition, decency, and the likely propagation of fundamental imbalances. Moral artificial intelligence professionals in law enforcement advocate for straightforwardness in algorithmic navigation, normal reviews to recognize and amend predispositions, and progressing assessment of the cultural effect of artificial intelligence frameworks. Finding some kind of harmony between the utilization of computer based intelligence for public wellbeing and the security of individual freedoms is a moral basic in the law enforcement area.

The worldwide idea of simulated intelligence advances requires moral contemplations that rise above individual lines. Worldwide joint effort and the advancement of worldwide moral norms are critical for guaranteeing reliable and capable computer based intelligence rehearses. Moral dynamic in simulated intelligence includes drawing in with assorted viewpoints, regarding social subtleties, and tending to worldwide difficulties altogether.

Drives that advance cooperation between states, industry, the scholarly world, and common society add to the foundation of moral standards that guide the mindful organization of simulated intelligence on a worldwide scale.

In the field of medical care, where artificial intelligence navigation has groundbreaking potential, moral contemplations spin around tolerant independence, information protection, and the dependable utilization of clinical information. Moral artificial intelligence rehearses focus on quiet prosperity, informed assent, and the straightforward correspondence of how artificial intelligence frameworks add to clinical choices. Finding some kind of harmony between utilizing artificial intelligence for clinical headways and maintaining moral standards is pivotal for keeping up with trust in medical services frameworks.

The moral ramifications of simulated intelligence dynamic in schooling require cautious consideration, especially with regards to understudy evaluations, customized learning, and the potential for predisposition in calculations. Moral contemplations include guaranteeing that artificial intelligence frameworks contribute emphatically to instructive results, advance reasonableness and inclusivity, and regard the freedoms of understudies. Moral dynamic in schooling incorporates progressing assessment, straightforwardness in algorithmic cycles, and a pledge to tending to any potentially negative side-effects or predispositions.

A basic moral thought in man-made intelligence direction is the potential for unseen side-effects. Artificial intelligence frameworks work in view of the information they are prepared on, and startling results might emerge, particularly in complicated, powerful conditions. Moral simulated intelligence professionals underline persistent checking, thorough testing, and the joining of criticism circles to recognize and address potentially negative results. The moral obligation lies in limiting the dangers related with computer based intelligence direction and being receptive to arising difficulties.

Public commitment and cooperation in the dynamic cycle encompassing artificial intelligence advancements are basic for guaranteeing that assorted points of view are thought of. Moral simulated intelligence rehearses include making roads for public talk, consolidating criticism from impacted networks, and encouraging a popularity based way to deal with the turn of events and sending of computer based intelligence frameworks. Public mindfulness crusades, instructive drives, and comprehensive gatherings for conversation add to moral dynamic that mirrors the qualities and worries of society.

Chapter 4

Adapting to Workplace Transformation

In the steadily developing scene of the cutting edge work environment, the idea of transformation has become inseparable from endurance. As businesses go through extremist changes driven by innovative headways, globalization, and moving financial ideal models, people and associations the same end up exploring strange regions. The speed of progress is persevering, and the people who neglect to adjust risk being abandoned following advancement.

Working environment change is a diverse peculiarity that envelops changes in hierarchical designs, mechanical reconciliation, social movements, and worker assumptions. Exploring this intricate landscape requires an all encompassing methodology that perceives the interconnectedness of these different components. Fruitful variation to working environment change includes a fragile harmony between embracing development and safeguarding guiding principle, between utilizing state of the art innovations and keeping a human-driven center.

One of the main thrusts behind working environment change is the fast headway of innovation. The advanced age has introduced a time of exceptional availability and robotization, reshaping the manner in which organizations work. From man-made consciousness and AI to the Web of Things, associations are saddling the force of innovation to smooth out processes, improve efficiency, and gain an upper hand. Therefore, workers are expected to foster new ranges of abilities and adjust to an always changing innovative scene.

The combination of innovation into the work environment isn't without its difficulties. Protection from change is a characteristic human nature, and numerous representatives may at first be troubled about taking on new innovations. To beat this opposition, associations should put resources into far reaching preparing programs and make a culture that encourages an inspirational perspective towards mechanical development. Representatives ought to be engaged with the information and abilities expected to unhesitatingly explore the advanced scene.

Close by mechanical headways, work environment change is in many cases set apart by a rebuilding of hierarchical ordered progressions. Conventional hierarchical designs are giving way to additional adaptable and cooperative models that support open correspondence and thought sharing. This shift mirrors an acknowledgment of the worth of different points of view and the requirement for dexterity in answering quickly changing business sector elements.

Be that as it may, rebuilding alone isn't adequate. Associations should likewise develop a steady and comprehensive culture that esteems the commitments of each and every colleague. This expects administration to support variety and consideration drives, cultivating a climate where representatives feel enabled to communicate their thoughts and assessments unafraid of retaliation. In the changed working environment, variety isn't simply a popular expression; an essential basic drives development and versatility.

Social change is a key part of working environment variation. As associations advance, so too should their social standards and values. Pioneers assume an essential part in molding and conveying the hierarchical culture, establishing the vibe for how workers connect and team up. Straightforwardness, trust, and a common feeling of direction are vital components of a good working environment culture that works with variation.

Viable correspondence is a vital part of social change. Pioneers should convey the reasoning behind changes, tending to any worries or vulnerabilities that might emerge among workers. Straightforward correspondence fabricates trust and assists workers with figuring out the more extensive vision of the association, encouraging a feeling of arrangement and mutual perspective.

The changed working environment is described by an emphasis on results instead of simple result. In conventional settings, achievement was much of the time estimated by the quantity of hours worked or assignments finished. Interestingly, the cutting edge work environment values results, empowering representatives to zero in on accomplishing objectives and making significant commitments. This shift requires a reconsideration of execution measurements and a move towards result driven evaluations.

To work with this change, associations ought to put resources into execution the board frameworks that accentuate joint effort, nonstop criticism, and individual turn of events. Standard registrations and useful criticism meetings empower workers to grasp their assets and regions for development, encouraging a culture of ceaseless learning and improvement.

Adaptability is a foundation of work environment change. The inflexible all day working day is progressively giving way to adaptable timetables, remote work choices, and elective work plans. The Coronavirus pandemic sped up this shift, featuring the possibility and advantages of remote work. Accordingly, associations are reexamining their way to deal with work plans, perceiving the significance of giving adaptability to draw in and hold top ability.

Remote work, be that as it may, brings its own arrangement of difficulties. Keeping a feeling of association and brotherhood among remote groups requires deliberate endeavors from initiative. Virtual group building exercises, standard video meetings, and open channels of correspondence assist with overcoming any issues made by actual distance. Associations should likewise put resources into innovation that works with consistent joint effort and guarantees that distant representatives have the devices they should be useful.

In the changed working environment, initiative takes on another aspect. The various leveled, definitive authority style of the past is giving way to additional comprehensive and versatile types of administration. Pioneers are supposed to motivate and engage their groups, encouraging a cooperative climate where different thoughts are invited and esteemed. The capacity to understand anyone on a profound level, sympathy, and the capacity to explore vagueness are turning out to be progressively significant initiative qualities.

Pioneers should likewise be light-footed in their direction, ready to turn rapidly in light of evolving conditions. The capacity to embrace vulnerability and lead with flexibility is fundamental in a working environment described by fast change. Comprehensive initiative, which esteems the special commitments of each colleague, is significant for building a firm and persuaded labor force in the changed working environment.

The versatility of representatives is a basic calculate the outcome of work environment change. The conventional thought of a direct vocation way is advancing, and representatives should be ready to embrace an outlook of persistent mastering and expertise improvement. Deep rooted learning is as of now not an extravagance yet a need, as innovation and market requests develop at an extraordinary speed.

Associations can uphold worker flexibility by putting resources into powerful preparation and improvement programs. Upskilling and reskilling drives guarantee that representatives stay furnished with the abilities expected to flourish in the changed work environment. Moreover, cultivating a learning society where interest and development are supported establishes a climate where representatives feel persuaded to investigate novel thoughts and approaches.

In the changed working environment, the job of HR is going through a critical shift. HR capabilities are not generally restricted to managerial errands yet assume an essential part in driving hierarchical change and supporting worker improvement. HR experts should be proactive in expecting the advancing requirements of the labor force and carrying out arrangements and practices that work with variation.

Representative prosperity is a focal point of HR in the changed work environment. The acknowledgment that representative wellbeing and joy contribute straightforwardly to efficiency and development has prompted a reexamination of work environment health programs. Past actual wellbeing, associations are progressively focusing on emotional well-being drives, perceiving the effect of pressure and burnout on by and large prosperity.

The utilization of information and examination is one more element of HR change. Individuals examination empowers HR experts to accumulate experiences into representative way of behaving, execution, and commitment. This information driven approach permits associations to settle on informed conclusions about ability the board, distinguish regions for development, and streamline their human resources techniques.

Working environment change is definitely not a one-size-fits-all undertaking. Every association is remarkable, with its own arrangement of difficulties, valuable open doors, and social subtleties. Redoing the way to deal with change is fundamental for progress. This includes directing an exhaustive evaluation of the association's present status, distinguishing regions that require consideration, and fostering a custom-made system for transformation.

Change the board turns into a basic part of work environment change. Successfully overseeing change requires clear correspondence, partner commitment, and a staged way to deal with execution. Workers ought to be engaged with the interaction, with potential open doors for criticism and info. By cultivating a feeling of pride and contribution, associations can moderate obstruction and fabricate support for the progressions ahead.

Nonstop checking and assessment are fundamental parts of work environment change. As changes are executed, associations should follow their effect, gathering input from representatives and surveying the adequacy of new arrangements and practices. This iterative interaction considers changes and refinements, guaranteeing that the change venture stays on track.

Cooperation is a vital driver of progress in the changed work environment. Storehouses and departmental obstructions impede development and nimbleness. Associations should separate these obstructions, encouraging a culture of coordinated effort where cross-practical groups can team up consistently. Innovation assumes a urgent part in empowering coordinated effort, giving devices and stages that work with correspondence and information sharing.

4.1 Remote Work: Automation's Catalyst

The scene of work is going through a significant change, and at the core of this development lies the rising predominance of remote work. A seismic shift has happened, advanced by innovative headways and the worldwide reaction to the Coronavirus pandemic. Remote work has risen above its status as a brief arrangement, arising as a drawn out worldview that is reshaping the manner in which people and associations conceptualize work, coordinated effort, and efficiency.

At the center of this remote work upheaval is the unavoidable impact of mechanization. Robotization, driven by man-made brainpower (simulated intelligence) and mechanical innovations, has turned into an impetus for the extension and enhancement of remote work capacities. The collaboration between remote work and computerization is changing the conventional work model, offering additional opportunities, efficiencies, and difficulties that request consideration and transformation.

The ascent of remote work is definitely not a simple result of mechanical progression; it mirrors a more extensive change in cultural qualities and assumptions. The craving for more noteworthy balance between serious and fun activities, adaptability, and independence has filled the interest for remote work choices. Associations, thusly, are perceiving the advantages of taking advantage of a worldwide ability pool, lessening topographical requirements, and cultivating a more comprehensive workplace.

Computerization, with its capacity to smooth out errands, improve productivity, and increase human abilities, adjusts flawlessly with the objectives of remote work. The assembly of these patterns is reshaping the actual idea of work, testing conventional thoughts of office-centricity and reclassifying the limits among expert and individual life. As we dig into the mind boggling connection between remote work and computerization, it becomes clear that the incorporation of these two powers isn't simply a reaction to outer conditions yet a purposeful and extraordinary decision molding the eventual fate of work.

One of the essential drivers behind the remote work insurgency is the advancement of correspondence and joint effort innovations. The appearance of high velocity web, distributed computing, and a heap of coordinated effort instruments has made it feasible for groups to work consistently across geological distances. Video conferencing, project the executives programming, and virtual joint effort stages have become fundamental parts of the remote work tool compartment, encouraging constant correspondence and cooperation.

Mechanization supplements these advances via robotizing normal and redundant errands, permitting workers to zero in on higher-esteem, vital exercises. As normal errands are offloaded to computerized frameworks, telecommuters can commit their significant investment to inventive critical thinking, development, and undertakings that require a human touch.

This harmonious connection between remote work innovations and robotization improves in general efficiency and adds to a more significant and drawing in work insight.

The reconciliation of computerization in remote work is most apparent in the domain of routine and rule-based assignments. Dreary cycles that once consumed critical parts of the business day can now be effectively taken care of by wise computerization frameworks. Whether it's information section, record handling, or client support requests, mechanization advances like mechanical cycle computerization (RPA) and chatbots have arisen as significant resources in the remote work scene.

This shift towards task mechanization has suggestions for work jobs and ability necessities. As normal undertakings become computerized, the interest for abilities, for example, decisive reasoning, critical thinking, and the capacity to understand people on a deeper level turns out to be more articulated. Telecommuters are progressively expected to carry a special human point of view to their jobs, underscoring imagination and flexibility — the very characteristics that put people aside from machines.

The democratization of remote work, empowered via mechanization, has prompted a reconsidering of ability securing and labor force variety. Associations are not generally limited by topographical limitations while obtaining ability. Remote work permits them to take advantage of a worldwide ability pool, getting to people with different abilities and points of view. This borderless way to deal with ability securing isn't just a shelter for associations yet in addition a chance to cultivate inclusivity and variety in the labor force.

Nonetheless, as remote work turns out to be more predominant, associations should address the potential difficulties related with mechanization. One concern is the effect on work dislodging. While robotization smoothes out cycles and lifts proficiency, it might prompt the reexamination of specific jobs. Associations must proactively deal with this progress by giving reskilling and upskilling open doors to representatives, guaranteeing they can adjust to advancing position necessities.

Additionally, the dependence on computerization acquaints contemplations related with information security and protection. As telecommuters access and offer delicate data from different areas, associations should carry out powerful network safety measures to defend information. This involves an extensive methodology that incorporates secure correspondence channels, information encryption, and worker preparing on network safety best practices.

The developing idea of work, described by far off coordinated effort and expanded dependence on robotization, requires a reexamination of customary execution measurements. Associations are creating some distance from estimating achievement exclusively founded on time spent in the workplace.

All things being equal, the center is moving towards result driven execution evaluations. This shift lines up with the inherent characteristics of remote work, accentuating results and commitments over actual presence.

Execution the executives in a remote workplace benefits from the coordination of mechanization through information examination. Robotized instruments can give experiences into representative execution, featuring accomplishments, regions for development, and potential advancement open doors. This information driven approach permits associations to arrive at informed conclusions about ability the executives and engages workers with customized input.

The adaptability presented by remote work is a situation with two sides. While it furnishes representatives with independence over their plans for getting work done, it likewise obscures the limits among expert and individual life. The "consistently on" culture, exacerbated by the steady availability worked with by computerized instruments, presents difficulties to worker prosperity. Associations should be mindful of the potential for burnout and stress among telecommuters.

Robotization can assume a part in moderating these difficulties. Via computerizing routine errands and upgrading work processes, associations can assist with reducing the weight on representatives and establish a better workplace. Furthermore, robotization can be utilized to screen responsibilities, recognize expected indications of burnout, and work with mediations to help representative prosperity. Finding some kind of harmony among adaptability and limits is fundamental for encouraging a practical remote work model.

As associations embrace the remote work worldview, the idea of the actual office goes through a change. The customary office, when seen as the focal point of work, is developing into a center for cooperation, development, and social connection. The workplace turns into a space where representatives meet up for up close and personal gatherings, meetings to generate new ideas, and group building exercises, instead of a required day to day objective.

Robotization adds to this shift by empowering associations to streamline office spaces for coordinated effort and imagination. With routine errands robotized and a critical piece of the labor force working from a distance, associations can reconsider office designs to encourage joint effort and development. Insightful computerization frameworks can be coordinated into the actual climate, giving a consistent encounter to representatives progressing among remote and office work.

The remote work insurgency, driven via mechanization, has suggestions for initiative and authoritative culture. Pioneers should adjust their administration styles to lead remote groups actually. The accentuation shifts from checking hours attempted to setting clear assumptions, encouraging a culture of trust, and supporting representative turn of events.

Fruitful far off initiative requires an emphasis on results, successful correspondence, and the capacity to explore the subtleties of virtual cooperation.

Hierarchical culture assumes a urgent part in the progress of remote work drives. A culture that values independence, joint effort, and results establishes a climate where remote work can flourish. Pioneers should effectively develop a feeling of having a place among distant representatives, cultivating a common vision and values that rise above actual limits. Computerization, by smoothing out processes and upgrading effectiveness, adds to a positive remote work culture by limiting grating and empowering smooth joint effort.

The remote work and robotization cooperative energy stretches out past customary business models, bringing about the gig economy and adaptable work courses of action. Specialists, self employed entities, and gig laborers influence advanced stages to somewhat offer their abilities and administrations. Computerization stages empower these specialists to get to valuable open doors, oversee projects, and convey brings about a decentralized way.

The gig economy, powered by remote work and robotization, offers the two open doors and difficulties. From one perspective, it furnishes people with the adaptability to pick their tasks and work on a time-table that suits their way of life. Then again, it brings up issues about professional stability, benefits, and the developing idea of the business worker relationship. Associations should explore this scene cautiously, guaranteeing that gig laborers are dealt with decently and impartially.

4.2 Redefining Job Structures in Automated Industries

The determined walk of robotization and man-made reasoning (simulated intelligence) has generally modified the scene of ventures around the world, inciting an exhaustive reconsideration of occupation designs and jobs. The appearance of trend setting innovations has introduced a time where machines and calculations are progressively equipped for performing undertakings customarily completed by human laborers. This shift isn't simply a mechanical development yet an extraordinary power that requires a redefinition of how we conceptualize, put together, and esteem work in computerized ventures.

One of the characterizing elements of robotized businesses is the combination of advanced mechanics and computer based intelligence frameworks into different features of creation and administration conveyance. From assembling plants to client support tasks, computerization has turned into an inescapable power, carrying with it expanded proficiency, accuracy, and versatility. Be that as it may, the ascent of mechanization suggests significant conversation starters about the idea of human work and the job of representatives in a scene overwhelmed by machines.

The effect of robotization on work structures is multi-layered. Normal and dreary errands that are powerless to robotization are progressively being performed by machines, prompting a reconfiguration of occupation jobs. This shift isn't restricted to low-talented positions; even exceptionally concentrated undertakings are not safe to mechanization. As machines assume control over routine capabilities, human specialists are freed to zero in on more mind boggling, imaginative, and esteem driven parts of their jobs.

One of the vital drivers of this change is the increase of human capacities through computerization. Instead of survey computerization as a danger to occupations, seeing it as a device that improves the capacities of human workers is more useful. Computer based intelligence frameworks can investigate huge datasets, distinguish designs, and perform complex estimations at speeds a long ways past human limit. By appointing these assignments to machines, human specialists can use their mental capacities for errands that require the ability to understand individuals on a deeper level, decisive reasoning, and complex critical thinking.

The idea of "cross breed" or "increased" positions is arising as a reaction to the mix of robotization. In these jobs, people work together consistently with smart machines, making a cooperative relationship that profits by the qualities of both. For instance, in medical care, simulated intelligence frameworks can break down clinical pictures for irregularities, permitting medical care experts to zero in on finding and patient consideration. Additionally, in assembling, robots can deal with dreary undertakings, while human laborers direct quality control, advancement, and the improvement of creation processes.

This redefinition of occupation structures requires a change in outlook in schooling and abilities improvement. The abilities expected in the robotized ventures representing things to come stretch out past specialized capability in unambiguous undertakings. There is a rising interest for abilities that machines see as trying to duplicate, like inventiveness, versatility, the capacity to appreciate individuals at their core, and complex critical thinking. Instructive foundations and preparing programs should advance to outfit the labor force with the abilities expected to flourish in jobs that influence human qualities close by mechanization.

The computerization of businesses additionally leads to the requirement for constant learning and upskilling. As advances develop, so do the ability necessities. Workers in computerized enterprises should be proactive in keeping up to date with mechanical progressions and getting new abilities. Deep rooted learning turns into a foundation of progress, with associations putting resources into powerful preparation projects to guarantee their labor force stays lithe and equipped for exploring the consistently changing scene of robotized ventures.

One more feature of the reclassified work structures is the rise of interdisciplinary jobs. As mechanization obscures the limits between customary work classes, representatives are progressively expected to have a mix of abilities from different fields.

For example, a job in information examination might require a mix of measurable mastery, programming abilities, and space explicit information. This interdisciplinary methodology mirrors the interconnected idea of errands in computerized ventures and the requirement for representatives who can connect holes between various subject matters.

Nonetheless, the coordination of computerization additionally raises worries about work removal and the fate of work. As machines assume control over routine undertakings, there is a real trepidation that specific work classes might decrease, prompting joblessness in unambiguous areas. Tending to this challenge requires a proactive methodology from states, associations, and instructive organizations. Drives, for example, reskilling programs, labor force progress support, and the production of new position open doors are fundamental parts of a thorough technique to moderate the effect of computerization on business.

Additionally, the moral ramifications of robotization should be painstakingly thought of. As machines assume a more conspicuous part in dynamic cycles, issues connected with straightforwardness, responsibility, and predisposition become basic. Associations should guarantee that mechanized frameworks are planned and carried out morally, with components set up to address unseen side-effects and shield against prejudicial results. Moreover, the moral utilization of information, protection concerns, and the cultural effect of robotization require insightful thought and guideline.

With regards to computerized businesses, influential positions likewise go through a change. Pioneers are entrusted with exploring the intricacies of human-machine cooperation, encouraging a culture of development, and guaranteeing the moral sending of mechanization. The capacity to lead in a climate where human specialists and wise machines coincide is a particular range of abilities. Compelling forerunners in computerized ventures should be capable at overseeing change, motivating a feeling of direction, and working with persistent learning and variation.

The re-imagined work structures in robotized businesses stretch out past the customary business model. The ascent of the gig economy, portrayed by present moment, project-based work worked with by advanced stages, is firmly entwined with the robotization peculiarity. Specialists and self employed entities influence their abilities in different activities, frequently empowered via robotization apparatuses that smooth out project the board, correspondence, and cooperation.

The gig economy presents the two amazing open doors and difficulties. On one hand, it offers people the adaptability to pick their ventures, work on a timetable that suits their inclinations, and access a different scope of chances.

Then again, inquiries concerning professional stability, benefits, and the obscuring of customary business representative connections come to the front. Associations should explore this scene cautiously, guaranteeing that gig laborers are dealt with reasonably, with contemplations for their prosperity and expert turn of events.

The re-imagined work structures in computerized businesses likewise have suggestions for authoritative designs. The various leveled, siloed models of the past are giving way to additional adaptable, deft designs that work with coordinated effort and advancement. Cross-practical groups, enabled via computerization instruments, work cooperatively to take care of perplexing issues and drive authoritative achievement. This shift towards compliment hierarchical designs is a reaction to the requirement for deftness and quick dynamic in the unique scene of mechanized enterprises.

Coordinated effort turns into a foundation of outcome in the reclassified work designs of robotized ventures. Human specialists and wise machines should team up flawlessly to accomplish ideal results. This requires a social shift inside associations, cultivating a climate where cooperation is supported, and various points of view are esteemed. Advancements that work with virtual cooperation, project the board, and correspondence make light of a significant job in breaking hindrances and empowering powerful collaboration.

The effect of robotization on work structures isn't uniform across ventures. While specific areas experience huge disturbances, others witness the rise of new open doors. For instance, businesses vigorously dependent on routine errands, for example, assembling and client support, go through significant changes as these undertakings become robotized. On the other side, ventures that influence computerization for development, information examination, and exploration experience a flood popular for gifted experts who can explore the intricacies of keen frameworks.

In the medical care industry, for example, mechanization adds to more exact diagnostics, customized therapy designs, and smoothed out managerial cycles. Savvy frameworks break down persistent information, distinguish examples, and help medical care experts in going with informed choices. While computerization smoothes out routine assignments, it upgrades the abilities of medical care experts, permitting them to zero in on persistent consideration, research, and the advancement of creative clinical arrangements.

The reconciliation of computerization in the monetary area is one more illustration of how occupation structures are being reclassified. Computerized frameworks handle routine exchanges, misrepresentation discovery, and chance evaluation, opening up human specialists to zero in on vital monetary preparation, relationship the board, and administrative consistence. The cooperative energy between human ability and machine proficiency is reshaping the monetary business' work scene.

In the field of training, mechanization devices add to customized opportunities for growth, information examination for execution appraisals, and managerial effectiveness. Instructors can use insightful frameworks to fit instructive substance to individual understudy needs, while managerial assignments are smoothed out through computerization. The job of instructors advances to incorporate mentorship, innovativeness.

4.3 Upskilling and Reskilling Initiatives in the Automated Era

The fast progression of innovation, especially in the domains of computerized reasoning (man-made intelligence) and robotization, has introduced another time where the abilities requested by the gig market are ceaselessly developing. As machines take on routine errands, the idea of work is going through a huge change, requiring a change in perspective in the abilities that people need to flourish in the cutting edge labor force. In this unique situation, upskilling and reskilling drives have arisen as significant procedures for engaging the current and future labor force to adjust to the requests of the robotized time.

The Basic for Upskilling and Reskilling

The speed of innovative change is phenomenal, and it brings the two open doors and difficulties. Robotization, AI, and artificial intelligence can possibly reform enterprises, expanding productivity and advancement. Nonetheless, this influx of robotization likewise can possibly disturb customary work jobs, delivering specific abilities outdated while encouraging interest for new, more particular ones. To address this test, people and associations the same should embrace an outlook of ceaseless mastering and expertise improvement.

Upskilling alludes to the method involved with procuring new abilities to improve one's ongoing capacities. This includes expanding after existing capabilities to remain significant and cutthroat in a quickly changing position market. Then again, reskilling includes learning an altogether new arrangement of abilities, frequently because of movements in industry requests or the presentation of new advances that render current abilities old.

The Job of Innovation in Learning Drives

Innovation assumes a significant part in the conveyance and openness of upskilling and reskilling drives. Web based learning stages, Gigantic Open Web-based Courses (MOOCs), and virtual homerooms have become indispensable parts of these drives, giving adaptable and versatile approaches to people to procure new abilities. These stages influence media content, intuitive activities, and computer experiences to make vivid growth opportunities, taking care of an extensive variety of learning styles.

The utilization of simulated intelligence in learning stages is especially imperative. Versatile learning frameworks controlled by simulated intelligence can customize growth opportunities in view of individual advancement and inclinations. These frameworks examine information on how clients draw in with content, recognize solid areas and shortcoming, and designer the learning excursion to suit every individual's necessities.

This degree of personalization upgrades the viability of upskilling and reskilling programs, guaranteeing that students get designated guidance in regions where they need it most.

In addition, arising advances like computer generated simulation (VR) and expanded reality (AR) are tracking down applications in expertise improvement. VR, for instance, can mimic genuine situations, giving students a pragmatic, active involvement with a protected and controlled climate. This is especially important in enterprises where active experience is significant, like medical care, assembling, and crisis administrations.

Industry Joint effort and Associations

In the robotized time, cooperation between instructive establishments, industry players, and innovation suppliers becomes basic. The conventional schooling system is frequently tested to stay up with quickly changing ability necessities. Cooperative endeavors that unite the scholarly world, organizations, and innovation specialists can overcome this issue, guaranteeing that instructive projects line up with the necessities of the gig market.

Organizations among organizations and instructive foundations can take different structures, including temporary positions, apprenticeships, and joint educational program improvement. These drives empower understudies and laborers to acquire useful experience while remaining sensitive to the most recent industry patterns. By effectively including industry experts in the plan and conveyance of instructive projects, organizations can guarantee that their contributions are applicable, useful, and lined up with true requests.

Innovation organizations likewise assume a pivotal part in upskilling and reskilling drives. They frequently give the stages, devices, and assets expected to convey top caliber, tech-empowered opportunities for growth. Cooperation between innovation suppliers and instructive foundations guarantees that the framework supporting upskilling endeavors is hearty, versatile, and fit for conveying a consistent opportunity for growth to an expansive crowd.

Government Drives and Strategy Backing

Legislatures overall perceive the significance of upskilling and reskilling even with robotization. Strategies and drives pointed toward encouraging a culture of consistent learning and flexibility are key parts of labor force improvement techniques. States might offer monetary motivating forces, tax reductions, or appropriations to the two people and organizations participated in upskilling and reskilling exercises.

Public-private organizations are one more road through which state run administrations can uphold upskilling drives. By teaming up with organizations, instructive foundations, and non-benefit associations, states can use a different arrangement of assets to address the expertise holes common in their economies.

Such organizations empower the plan and execution of thorough upskilling programs that take care of the particular requirements of various businesses.

Moreover, legislatures can put resources into establishing a favorable administrative climate that works with upskilling and reskilling. This might include perceiving and authorizing forward thinking learning pathways, empowering the acknowledgment of advanced identifications or miniature accreditations as marks of abilities dominance, and advancing the utilization of inventive learning procedures.

The Change in Abilities Request

The abilities requested by the gig market in the computerized period are going through a principal shift. While specialized abilities connected with information examination, programming, and man-made intelligence are popular, there is a rising accentuation on what are frequently alluded to as "delicate abilities" or "21st-century abilities." These incorporate decisive reasoning, innovativeness, the capacity to understand individuals at their core, flexibility, and complex critical thinking.

The capacity to work cooperatively and impart actually is becoming foremost. As robotization assumes control over routine errands, human laborers are supposed to succeed in regions where machines presently battle, for example, understanding nuanced human feelings, exploring complex relational elements, and practicing imagination in critical thinking. Upskilling and reskilling drives must, consequently, address this more extensive range of abilities to guarantee that people are prepared to flourish in the developing work environment.

Inclusivity and Availability

Guaranteeing that upskilling and reskilling valuable open doors are comprehensive and available to all portions of society is a critical thought. The advanced gap, which alludes to variations in admittance to innovation and the web, can make obstructions to support in web based learning drives. Addressing these inconsistencies requires purposeful endeavors to give reasonable web access, gadgets, and advanced proficiency preparing to underserved populaces.

Moreover, upskilling and reskilling projects ought to be intended to oblige different learning styles, inclinations, and instructive foundations. Forward thinking students, incorporating those with work experience yet deficient with regards to formal capabilities, ought to have pathways to get new abilities and certifications. Adaptable learning designs, acknowledgment of earlier learning, and the acknowledgment of elective certifications are fundamental parts of making a comprehensive upskilling biological system.

The Job of Managers in Upskilling

Managers assume an essential part in driving upskilling and reskilling drives inside their associations. As the idea of work develops, managers should adopt a proactive strategy to distinguish the abilities their labor force needs both now and later on. This includes directing abilities hole evaluations, understanding arising industry drifts, and adjusting preparing projects to authoritative objectives.

Organizations can boost and support representative upskilling by offering learning open doors during work hours, giving monetary help to instruction, or laying out associations with instructive foundations. Making a culture that values nonstop mastering and expertise improvement cultivates a climate where representatives feel engaged to upgrade their capacities, adding to both individual vocation development and hierarchical flexibility.

Notwithstanding formal preparation programs, work environment learning through mentorship, peer cooperation, and hands on preparing is important. This experiential learning approach permits representatives to apply recently gained abilities in true situations, supporting their comprehension and adequacy.

Estimating the Effect of Upskilling Drives

Actually estimating the effect of upskilling and reskilling drives is fundamental for checking their prosperity and refining methodologies over the long haul. Key execution pointers (KPIs) may remember upgrades for individual and group efficiency, expanded development, a decrease in abilities holes, and improved worker fulfillment and maintenance.

Quantitative information on abilities securing, culmination rates, and execution enhancements give important bits of knowledge into the adequacy of upskilling programs. Studies and subjective criticism from members can offer a nuanced comprehension of the apparent effect on work fulfillment, profession movement, and the capacity to contribute definitively to the association.

Eventually, the progress of upskilling and reskilling drives ought to be estimated not just regarding individual and authoritative results yet additionally in their commitment to cultural flexibility and versatility despite mechanical change.

4.4 Balancing Flexibility and Security in Automated Work Environments

The coordination of mechanization into workplaces has introduced another period, changing how assignments are performed, and associations work. While robotization brings expanded proficiency, versatility, and development, it likewise presents a fragile harmony among adaptability and security. The need to figure out some kind of harmony is pivotal in guaranteeing that the benefits of computerization are augmented without compromising the uprightness of frameworks, information, and the general dependability of workplaces.

Adaptability in Computerized Workplaces

Adaptability in computerized workplaces alludes to the capacity of frameworks, cycles, and associations to adjust to evolving conditions, advancements, and requests. Robotization innately adds to adaptability by smoothing out work processes, decreasing manual mediation, and empowering fast acclimations to oblige moving needs. It permits associations to increase tasks or down proficiently, answer market changes quickly, and embrace dynamic plans of action.

One aspect of adaptability in robotized workplaces is the flexibility of representatives to advancing jobs and obligations. As normal undertakings become robotized, the labor force can turn towards more inventive, vital, and esteem driven exercises. This flexibility requires a culture that energizes constant getting the hang of, upskilling, and a mentality open to change. Representatives should be prepared to explore the developing scene of computerized work, embracing new innovations and refining their ranges of abilities.

Moreover, the adaptability acquainted via mechanization reaches out with the idea of remote work. Keen frameworks and computerized instruments empower representatives to team up consistently from different areas, cultivating a decentralized workplace. This adaptability in work game plans adds to further developed balance between fun and serious activities, admittance to a worldwide ability pool, and expanded flexibility even with unexpected disturbances, like the worldwide pandemic that sped up the reception of remote work.

Security Contemplations in Mechanized Workplaces

As associations embrace the advantages of mechanization and adaptability, security contemplations become vital. Computerized workplaces, with their interconnected frameworks and dependence on advanced innovations, present an extended assault surface for potential digital dangers. The joining of mechanization presents new places of weakness that malevolent entertainers might take advantage of, going from programming weaknesses to social designing strategies.

Information security is an essential worry in robotized workplaces. Robotization frequently includes the handling and stockpiling of huge volumes of delicate data. Safeguarding this information from unapproved access, information breaks, and cyberattacks is basic. Hearty encryption, access controls, and customary security reviews are fundamental parts of a complete information security system.

Besides, the interconnected idea of computerized frameworks requires an emphasis on network security. Online protection measures should reach out past individual gadgets to defend the whole organization foundation. Firewalls, interruption identification frameworks, and secure correspondence conventions are crucial components in bracing the organization against likely dangers.

Client verification and approval components are basic in guaranteeing that main approved work force can get to and control mechanized frameworks. Multifaceted validation, solid secret phrase strategies, and job based admittance controls add to a layered security approach, decreasing the gamble of unapproved access.

The security of computerization programming and calculations is another urgent perspective. Associations should focus on secure coding rehearses, routinely update programming to fix weaknesses, and direct intensive testing to recognize and correct expected shortcomings. Furthermore, taking into account the straightforwardness and reasonableness of computerized dynamic cycles is fundamental, as it helps with recognizing and tending to expected predispositions and moral worries.

Finding Some kind of harmony Among Adaptability and Security

The test lies in finding some kind of harmony among adaptability and security in mechanized workplaces. An unbending, excessively got framework could smother development, block work process productivity, and frustrate the versatility of the association. Then again, a profoundly adaptable yet deficiently got framework is helpless to digital dangers, information breaks, and functional interruptions that can have extensive outcomes.

To accomplish this equilibrium, associations should embrace a comprehensive way to deal with network protection that is coordinated into the texture of mechanized processes. This includes considering safety efforts at each phase of the robotization lifecycle, from the plan and execution of frameworks to their continuous support and observing. Here are key methodologies for accomplishing this equilibrium:

Thorough Gamble Appraisal:

Leading a careful gamble evaluation is the groundwork of a versatile network protection methodology. This includes distinguishing possible dangers, weaknesses, and the expected effect of safety breaks. Associations should assess the dangers related with the particular advances and cycles associated with their computerized workplaces.

Versatile Security Arrangements:

Security arrangements ought to be versatile and receptive to the developing scene of digital dangers. This incorporates consistently refreshing strategies to address arising gambles, consolidating illustrations gained from security episodes, and guaranteeing that safety efforts line up with the association's evolving needs.

Worker Preparing and Mindfulness:

Human variables are a huge component in the security condition. Representatives should be taught on network safety best practices, the dangers related with computerized frameworks, and the job they play in keeping a protected workplace.

Preparing projects ought to cover points, for example, perceiving phishing endeavors, protecting certifications, and detailing security episodes quickly.

Nonstop Observing and Occurrence Reaction:

Nonstop observing of computerized frameworks is fundamental for recognizing potential security occurrences progressively. Robotized instruments for interruption discovery, log examination, and inconsistency identification can give early alerts of likely dangers. Moreover, associations should have a distinct occurrence reaction plan set up, framing the moves toward be taken in case of a security episode.

Encryption and Information Protection:

Encryption is a major safety effort for safeguarding touchy information on the way and very still. Associations should carry out strong encryption conventions to shield information from unapproved access.

Also, adherence to information protection guidelines is critical, guaranteeing that individual and delicate data is taken care of in consistence with lawful necessities.

Coordinated Security Practices:

In the soul of adaptability, security practices ought to be lithe and receptive to change. This includes integrating security contemplations into light-footed improvement processes, embracing DevSecOps standards, and coordinating security testing into the persistent mix/constant organization (CI/Compact disc) pipeline. Dexterous security rehearses empower associations to adjust rapidly to arising dangers and weaknesses.

Coordinated effort and Data Sharing:

Coordinated effort inside the business and data sharing about arising dangers and weaknesses can reinforce the general network safety act. Partaking in industry gatherings, sharing danger knowledge, and working together with friends can give significant experiences into advancing security gambles and powerful alleviation systems.

Moral Hacking and Entrance Testing:

Standard moral hacking and entrance testing can help associations distinguish and address expected shortcomings in their computerized frameworks. By mimicking genuine world cyberattacks, associations can proactively recognize weaknesses and carry out restorative estimates before pernicious entertainers exploit them.

Administrative Consistence:

Consistence with industry-explicit guidelines and norms is a primary component of a safe computerized workplace. Associations should remain informed about developing administrative prerequisites, guaranteeing that their computerized frameworks stick to the essential norms for security, security, and information assurance.

Secure Joint effort Devices:

The rising dependence on remote work requires the utilization of secure joint effort devices. Associations ought to pick devices that focus on start to finish encryption, secure correspondence channels, and strong access controls. This guarantees that cooperative workplaces stay adaptable yet impervious to potential security dangers.

The Human Component in Adjusting Adaptability and Security

While cutting edge innovations drive mechanization and add to the adaptability of workplaces, the human component stays key to the sensitive harmony among adaptability and security. Human way of behaving, mindfulness, and dynamic assume significant parts in deciding the adequacy of safety efforts.

Representative mindfulness programs, preparing drives, and a solid security culture are crucial parts of this human-driven approach. Representatives should comprehend the dangers related with their activities, be watchful against social designing assaults, and effectively add to keeping a protected workplace. Engaging workers to be proactive in recognizing and detailing security concerns improves the association's general security act.

Besides, including workers in the plan and execution of safety efforts cultivates a feeling of responsibility and responsibility. At the point when workers comprehend the reasoning behind security approaches and practices, they are bound to stick to them and add to the association's security goals.

Chapter 5

Upskilling Initiatives

In a time characterized by quick mechanical headways and developing position scenes, the requirement for upskilling has become more basic than any other time. Upskilling drives are instructive undertakings pointed toward upgrading the ranges of abilities of people, setting them up for the difficulties of the cutting edge labor force. As businesses go through groundbreaking changes, driven via robotization, man-made reasoning, and other troublesome innovations, the significance of remaining on the ball through persistent learning couldn't possibly be more significant.

The Changing Scene of Work

The idea of work is going through a significant change, impacted by variables like globalization, digitization, and the ascent of the gig economy. Customary work jobs are developing, and new ones are arising, requesting a different arrangement of abilities that go past the extent of ordinary schooling. Thus, there is a developing acknowledgment that the information procured in proper schooling may not do the trick for a long lasting profession.

One of the vital drivers behind the changing scene of work is the fast headway of innovation. Computerization and man-made reasoning are upsetting businesses, mechanizing routine errands and increasing human capacities. While this commitments expanded productivity and development, it likewise requires a labor force that is versatile and outfitted with the abilities expected to flourish in an innovation driven climate.

The Criticalness of Upskilling

As mechanical disturbances reshape enterprises, there is a critical requirement for people to upskill to stay important in the gig market. The World Financial Gathering's Eventual fate of Occupations report features the rising interest for abilities, for example, complex critical thinking, decisive reasoning, imagination, and the capacity to understand people on a profound level. These abilities, frequently alluded to as delicate abilities, supplement specialized mastery and are vital for exploring the intricacies of the cutting edge working environment.

Upskilling isn't just about obtaining new specialized abilities yet additionally about fostering a development mentality and a promise to constant learning. As occupation jobs become more unique and complex, people need to embrace a learning society that empowers them to adjust to developing prerequisites. Upskilling is certainly not a one-time occasion; it is a constant excursion of learning and improvement that stretches out all through one's vocation.

Corporate Drives for Upskilling

Perceiving the meaning of upskilling, numerous partnerships are carrying out drives to cultivate a culture of consistent advancing inside their associations. These drives envelop different techniques, going from formal preparation projects to casual learning open doors.

Formal Preparation Projects: Organizations are putting resources into organized preparing projects to confer explicit abilities pertinent to their industry. These projects might incorporate studios, classes, and online courses intended to improve specialized capability and information.

Interior Portability Projects: To address the changing necessities of the labor force and the association, organizations are progressively zeroing in on inside versatility. This includes working with the development of representatives across various jobs and divisions, furnishing them with the chance to procure new abilities and encounters.

Computerized Learning Stages: The computerized transformation has led to a plenty of internet learning stages that deal seminars on a large number of subjects. Many organizations are utilizing these stages to give representatives admittance to learning assets, permitting them to upskill at their own speed.

Cooperation with Instructive Establishments: A few enterprises are shaping organizations with instructive foundations to make custom-made programs that line up with industry needs. These coordinated efforts might include the improvement of particular courses or degree programs that outfit understudies with the abilities expected by the labor force.

Mentorship Projects: Mentorship assumes a urgent part in proficient turn of events. Organizations are laying out mentorship programs that pair experienced representatives with those looking to upskill. This works with information move as well as encourages a feeling of local area inside the association.

Government Drives and Approaches

State run administrations all over the planet are additionally perceiving the significance of upskilling even with innovative interruptions and are carrying out different drives and arrangements to address the abilities hole. These drives are pointed toward outfitting people with the abilities expected to take part definitively in the advanced economy.

Expertise Improvement Projects: States are putting resources into expertise improvement programs that target explicit enterprises or areas confronting a lack of talented laborers. These projects frequently include coordinated effort with industry partners to guarantee that the abilities being bestowed are in accordance with market requests.

Monetary Motivators: A few legislatures give monetary impetuses to the two people and organizations to support cooperation in up-skilling programs. This might incorporate tax cuts, sponsorships, or awards to counterbalance the expenses related with preparing and improvement.

Public Capabilities Structures: Laying out public capabilities systems is a typical way to deal with normalize and approve abilities. These systems give an organized method for evaluating and perceive the abilities procured through formal and casual means, advancing a more straightforward and adaptable expertise environment.

Apprenticeship Projects: Apprenticeships are getting momentum as compelling instruments for ability improvement. Legislatures are supporting apprenticeship programs that permit people to learn at work while procuring a compensation, giving a down to earth pathway to obtain industry-explicit abilities.

STEM Schooling Drives: Perceiving the rising interest for abilities in science, innovation, designing, and arithmetic (STEM), legislatures are advancing STEM training drives at different levels. These drives expect to develop an interest in STEM subjects since the beginning and plan people for professions in innovation driven fields.

The Job of Instructive Organizations

Instructive organizations, including colleges and professional instructional hubs, assume a critical part in the upskilling environment. These establishments are adjusting their educational plans and helping strategies to guarantee that graduates are outfitted with the abilities requested by the contemporary work market.

Curricular Corrections: To address the developing necessities of the labor force, instructive foundations are updating their educational programs to integrate a more prominent accentuation on pragmatic abilities, critical thinking, and decisive reasoning. This might include the presentation of new courses or the mix of true undertakings into existing projects.

Industry Joint efforts: Joint efforts between instructive establishments and ventures are turning out to be more pervasive. These organizations furnish understudies with openness to industry rehearses, involved insight, and bits of knowledge into latest things, making them more market-prepared upon graduation.

Temporary job and Center Projects: Entry level position and community programs are vital parts of numerous instructive projects. These drives permit understudies to apply hypothetical information in genuine settings, acquiring reasonable experience and fostering the abilities expected for their picked fields.

Adaptable Learning Models: Perceiving the assorted necessities of students, instructive establishments are embracing adaptable learning models. This incorporates offering parttime projects, online courses, and secluded certificates that empower people to seek after schooling while at the same time adjusting work and different responsibilities.

Long lasting Learning Backing: Instructive establishments are progressively seeing advancing as a deep rooted try. They are laying out components to help graduated class and experts in ceaseless upskilling, giving admittance to assets, organizing open doors, and vocation direction all through their expert process.

Difficulties and Contemplations

While upskilling drives hold enormous commitment, they are not without challenges. Addressing these difficulties is fundamental to guarantee the adequacy and inclusivity of upskilling programs.

Access and Moderateness: Guaranteeing fair admittance to upskilling potential open doors is a critical test. Factors like monetary imperatives, geological area, and instructive foundation can make hindrances to cooperation. Endeavors are expected to make upskilling programs reasonable and open to a different scope of people.

Innovative Obstructions: The computerized partition stays a worry, for certain people lacking admittance to the important innovation and web network for web based learning. Upskilling drives should consider ways of overcoming this issue, for example, giving admittance to innovation or creating elective learning designs.

Pertinence of Content: The fast speed of innovative change implies that the importance of abilities can immediately become outdated. Upskilling programs should be light-footed and consistently refreshed to line up with industry needs. Cooperation among businesses and instructive organizations is essential to keeping up to date with arising patterns.

Acknowledgment of Casual Learning: Casual learning, acquired through work insight, independent review, or other modern means, is frequently underestimated. Endeavors ought to be made to perceive and approve the abilities gained through casual channels, guaranteeing a more extensive and comprehensive way to deal with upskilling.

Social Shift: Embracing a culture of nonstop learning requires a mentality shift for people and associations the same. Beating protection from change and encouraging a proactive way to deal with upskilling require purposeful endeavors in administration, correspondence, and hierarchical culture.

5.1 The Need for Upskilling and Reskilling

In the present quickly developing worldwide scene, the requirement for upskilling and reskilling has become more basic than any time in recent memory. Innovative progressions, financial movements, and cultural changes are reshaping the work market at an exceptional speed, delivering conventional ranges of abilities outdated and driving an interest for new, specific skills. As we explore the intricacies of the 21st 100 years, people, organizations, and instructive foundations should perceive the basic of ceaseless learning and transformation.

The speeding up speed of mechanical development has changed enterprises, robotizing routine undertakings and increasing human abilities. Man-made brainpower, AI, and robotization are at this point not cutting edge ideas; they are the current reality. As mechanization assumes control over everyday practice and dreary undertakings, the idea of occupations is developing, expecting laborers to have a mix of specialized abilities, decisive reasoning, innovativeness, and versatility. Thus, the once static sets of responsibilities are presently liquid, requesting a labor force that can explore a dynamic and dubious climate.

Globalization has likewise assumed a critical part in reshaping the work market. Organizations currently work in an associated, related reality where data and assets stream flawlessly across borders. This interconnectedness brings the two amazing open doors and difficulties. On one hand, organizations can take advantage of a different ability pool and markets all over the planet. Then again, they face expanded rivalry and the need to adjust to assorted social, monetary, and administrative settings. In this specific situation, people should foster a worldwide mentality and diverse relational abilities to flourish in an internationalized working environment.

The Coronavirus pandemic further sped up the advanced change of ventures and featured the significance of remote work abilities. Associations that adjusted quickly to the remote work model displayed the meaning of computerized proficiency and virtual coordinated effort abilities.

As the limits among physical and computerized work areas obscure, people need to dominate advanced devices, network safety mindfulness, and far off joint effort stages to remain pertinent and useful.

The idea of a 'task for life' is progressively turning into a remnant of the past. The gig economy, independent work, and transient agreements are turning out to be more pervasive, expecting people to deal with their vocations as arrangement of abilities and encounters instead of depending on the security of a solitary work. This shift requests an outlook of ceaseless learning and a proactive way to deal with expertise improvement to stay coordinated in a task market described by ease.

Because of these movements, the conventional model of instruction is going through a change. Deep rooted learning is arising as a foundation for individual and expert turn of events. Instructive organizations, once seen as suppliers of information for a proper period, are developing into stages that help continuous expertise obtaining. Internet learning, miniature certifications, and adaptable course structures are turning out to be progressively well known, permitting people to procure designated abilities without focusing on long haul, customary degrees.

In any case, the obligation regarding upskilling and reskilling isn't exclusively on the shoulders of people. Managers assume a vital part in encouraging a culture of constant advancing inside their associations. Perceiving the worth of a talented and versatile labor force, organizations are putting resources into representative preparation programs, mentorship drives, and associations with instructive establishments. In doing as such, they upgrade their representatives' capacities as well as make a stronger and creative hierarchical culture.

States likewise bear an obligation to address the upskilling basic. Policymakers need to plan systems that work with the reconciliation of upskilling and reskilling drives into the more extensive training and business scene. Public-private associations can be instrumental in adjusting instructive educational plans to industry needs, guaranteeing that the labor force is outfitted with the abilities requested by the advancing position market.

The requirement for upskilling and reskilling isn't bound to a specific industry or segment. An all inclusive basic slices across areas and applies to laborers of any age and foundations. Youthful experts entering the work market need to develop a mentality of ceaseless gaining from the start of their vocations. Mid-vocation experts should adjust and gain new abilities to stay serious in their fields. Indeed, even those coming retirement can profit from upskilling, guaranteeing a smooth change into jobs that influence their experience while consolidating new innovations and techniques.

One of the basic parts of upskilling is the improvement of advanced education. In a period overwhelmed by innovation, the capacity to explore advanced apparatuses and stages is non-debatable. Advanced education goes past essential PC abilities; it includes a profound comprehension of data frameworks, information examination, and network safety. People should be adroit at utilizing innovation to upgrade efficiency, convey really, and access data in an undeniably digitalized world.

The fast development of innovation requires an equal development in instructive methodologies. Customary instructive models, with their decent educational programs and government sanctioned testing, are unfit to stay up with the unique requests of the cutting edge labor force. Instructive organizations need to embrace adaptable, versatile learning models that underscore critical thinking, decisive reasoning, and inventiveness. Project-based learning, interdisciplinary investigations, and genuine uses of information can all the more likely get ready understudies for the intricacies of the contemporary work market.

Upskilling and reskilling are not restricted to specialized abilities alone. Delicate abilities, frequently ignored yet profoundly esteemed by businesses, are similarly critical. Correspondence, collaboration, versatility, and the ability to appreciate anyone on a deeper level are progressively becoming differentiators in employing choices. As computerization assumes control over routine undertakings, the capacity to team up, advance, and explore complex relational elements turns out to be more basic than any other time. Instructive projects and preparing drives must, in this way, integrate the advancement of these fundamental delicate abilities into their educational plans.

The gig economy, described by momentary agreements and independent work, is reshaping the idea of business. People are progressively choosing adaptable work game plans that permit them to seek after different undertakings at the same time or switch among jobs and businesses. While the gig economy offers independence and assortment, it likewise requires an expanded range of abilities. Gig laborers should continually adjust to the requests of various tasks and ventures, requiring a serious level of dexterity and flexibility.

The idea of "mixture occupations" is acquiring noticeable quality, where people are supposed to perform errands that customarily fell under unmistakable work jobs. This obscuring of occupation limits expects laborers to have a more extensive range of abilities that traverses various disciplines. For example, a promoting proficient may have to comprehend information examination, and a product engineer might be supposed to have a grip of client experience plan. The capacity to coordinate information from different spaces is turning into an important resource in the contemporary work market.

While upskilling and reskilling are indispensable for individual profession movement, they likewise add to more extensive cultural objectives. A talented and versatile labor force is fundamental for financial development, development, and seriousness on the worldwide stage. Nations that focus on instruction and expertise improvement are better situated to explore financial vulnerabilities, draw in venture, and cultivate a culture of development. The aggregate upskilling of a populace can prompt a stronger and prosperous society.

The effect of upskilling reaches out past individual professions and public economies — it has suggestions for social versatility and consideration. Admittance to quality schooling and preparing open doors can overcome any barrier between the special and the underestimated, giving a pathway to people from different foundations to partake genuinely in the labor force. Upskilling drives must, in this way, be planned in light of inclusivity, guaranteeing that open doors for learning and professional success are available to all.

The eventual fate of work is set apart by vulnerability, yet it likewise holds enormous potential for the people who are ready to embrace change. As businesses develop, new open doors arise, provoking interest for abilities that might not have existed 10 years prior. The capacity to recognize arising patterns, expect expertise holes, and proactively get pertinent capabilities is a significant characteristic in this powerful scene.

The job of mentorship in upskilling and reskilling couldn't possibly be more significant. Old pros who have explored the intricacies of their individual enterprises can give priceless direction to those trying to improve their abilities. Mentorship programs, whether formal or casual, work with information move, organizing, and the improvement of a comprehensive comprehension of the business. Tutors share specialized skill as well as confer bits of knowledge into the unwritten standards and subtleties of their callings.

As the interest for upskilling develops, the significance of perceiving and approving gained abilities becomes clear. Customary qualifications, like degrees and affirmations, are as yet significant yet may not completely catch a singular's abilities. The ascent of option credentialing systems, like computerized identifications and miniature qualifications, permits people to grandstand explicit abilities and capabilities in a more granular and available way. This shift towards a more nuanced credentialing framework lines up with the secluded, on-request nature of contemporary learning.

The appearance of man-made consciousness (artificial intelligence) and mechanization brings up issues about the future work market and the expected relocation of specific jobs. While mechanization might kill a few routine errands, it likewise sets out open doors for the turn of events and the executives of man-made intelligence frameworks. Understanding the interchange between human capacities and simulated intelligence innovations is urgent.

Rather than dreading dislodging, people can zero in on procuring abilities that supplement simulated intelligence, like decisive reasoning, the capacity to understand anyone at their core, and moral thinking.

Moral contemplations in upskilling and reskilling are vital. As innovation progresses, moral issues connected with information protection, algorithmic inclination, and the effect of mechanization on business should be tended to. Instructive projects and preparing drives ought to integrate moral aspects, cultivating a feeling of obligation and mindfulness among students. Moreover, organizations need to focus on moral contemplations in their computer based intelligence and robotization systems, guaranteeing that the sending of innovation lines up with cultural qualities and standards.

The orientation aspect of upskilling and reskilling is a basic perspective that merits consideration. All things considered, certain businesses and jobs have been overwhelmed by one orientation, making orientation based ability holes. Endeavors to connect these holes should address specialized abilities as well as the cultural standards and predispositions that add to orientation differences. Empowering ladies to seek after professions in STEM (science, innovation, designing, and arithmetic) fields, for instance, requires destroying generalizations and giving steady conditions to ability improvement.

The difficulties presented by the requirement for upskilling and reskilling are not inconceivable, however they require purposeful endeavors from people, organizations, instructive foundations, and policy-makers. Embracing a mentality of deep rooted picking up, encouraging a culture of persistent improvement, and focusing on inclusivity are key parts of exploring the developing position market. As the Fourth Modern Upheaval unfurls, portrayed by the combination of advanced, natural, and actual innovations, the basic for upskilling and reskilling will just increase.

All in all, the requirement for upskilling and reskilling is an impression of the unique idea of the cutting edge world. Innovative headways, monetary movements, and cultural changes are reshaping the work market, requesting a labor force that is spry, versatile, and furnished with a different range of abilities. The customary model of schooling is developing to fulfill these needs, with a more prominent accentuation on deep rooted learning, computerized proficiency, and delicate abilities. People, organizations, and legislatures all assume urgent parts in tending to the upskilling basic, with mentorship, elective credentialing, and moral contemplations being fundamental parts of this groundbreaking excursion. As we explore the intricacies of the 21st 100 years, the capacity to learn, forget, and relearn will be the foundation of person

5.2 Innovative Approaches to Workforce Training

In the steadily developing scene of work and business, creative ways to deal with labor force preparing have become basic. The customary models of schooling and preparing are being tested by the quick speed of mechanical progression, changes in the idea of work, and the requirement for a more versatile and talented labor force. As associations endeavor to stay cutthroat and people try to upgrade their employability, investigating and carrying out creative ways to deal with labor force preparing has turned into an essential need.

One of the groundbreaking patterns in labor force preparing is the shift towards on the web and computerized learning stages. The pervasiveness of the web and the rising openness of computerized gadgets have made ready for an upset in the conveyance of instructive substance. Online courses, online classes, and virtual homerooms offer adaptability and comfort, permitting students to get to preparing materials from anyplace on the planet. This shift towards advanced learning tends to geological limitations as well as takes special care of the different learning styles and inclinations of people.

Microlearning is arising as a strong methodology inside the computerized learning scene. Rather than conventional extended courses, microlearning conveys content in little, engaged modules that are effectively absorbable. This arrangement reverberates well with the advanced labor force, which frequently faces time imperatives and favors learning in reduced down increases. Microlearning modules can be incorporated into day to day work schedules, empowering representatives to procure new abilities without disturbing their work process fundamentally.

Versatile learning advances are one more imaginative road in labor force preparing. These advances use calculations and information investigation to customize the growth opportunity in light of individual advancement, inclinations, and execution. By fitting substance to the particular requirements of students, versatile learning frameworks improve the productivity and adequacy of preparing programs. This approach guarantees that people get designated guidance, tending to their one of a kind holes in information and expertise.

Reproductions and computer generated reality (VR) advancements are changing how workers are prepared, particularly in enterprises where active experience is significant. Reproduced conditions repeat true situations, giving a gamble free space to students to rehearse and refine their abilities. VR makes this a stride further by submerging students in a PC produced climate, making a more reasonable and drawing in opportunity for growth. These advances are especially important in fields like medical care, avionics, and assembling, where active preparation is costly or strategically testing.

Gamification is adding a component of tomfoolery and contest to labor force preparing. By consolidating game-like components like focuses, identifications, and competitor lists, preparing programs become seriously captivating and charming. Gamification persuades students as well as encourages a feeling of contest and accomplishment, improving the general growth opportunity. This approach is especially successful in catching the consideration of more youthful ages entering the labor force, who are acquainted with intuitive and gamified conditions.

Peer learning and cooperative preparation strategies influence the aggregate information and experience of a gathering. Distributed learning urges representatives to share their bits of knowledge, abilities, and best practices with their associates. This approach advances a culture of consistent advancing inside the association and takes advantage of the abundance of inner mastery. Cooperative preparation, for example, bunch tasks and group based reproductions, improves collaboration and relational abilities while tending to explicit learning goals.

Notwithstanding inward preparation drives, outer organizations with instructive establishments and industry specialists are building up some forward momentum. Coordinated efforts with colleges, professional schools, and concentrated preparing suppliers offer associations the valuable chance to take advantage of state of the art information and assets. These organizations can take different structures, including redid preparing programs, joint exploration ventures, and temporary position open doors. By cultivating these outside connections, associations guarantee that their labor force remains sensitive to the most recent industry patterns and advancements.

The idea of a learning society inside associations is turning out to be progressively noticeable. A learning society values constant improvement and perspectives advancing as an essential resource. In such a culture, workers are urged to search out learning open doors, explore different avenues regarding groundbreaking thoughts, and offer their insight with partners. Initiative assumes a pivotal part in encouraging a learning society by establishing the vibe, dispensing assets for preparing drives, and perceiving and compensating a pledge to learning.

Computerized reasoning (simulated intelligence) is assuming a groundbreaking part in labor force preparing by empowering customized, information driven experiences. Simulated intelligence calculations can investigate huge measures of information to distinguish individual learning examples, qualities, and regions for development. This information driven approach permits associations to fit preparing projects to the particular necessities of every worker, boosting the effect of learning drives. Computer based intelligence fueled chatbots and remote helpers likewise offer moment help and direction, upgrading the general opportunity for growth.

In light of the developing interest for specialized abilities, coding bootcamps have arisen as escalated, momentary preparation programs that furnish people with coding and programming abilities. These bootcamps are intended to be vivid and involved, giving a pragmatic and sped up opportunity for growth. Perceiving the business interest for explicit specialized abilities, coding bootcamps frequently team up with managers to adjust their educational programs to current industry needs, guaranteeing that graduates are work prepared.

Cross-utilitarian preparation is separating storehouses inside associations by presenting representatives to various jobs and works. This approach goes past customary departmental limits, empowering representatives to foster an expansive range of abilities that traverses different regions. Cross-practical preparation upgrades cooperation, advances an all encompassing comprehension of the association, and gets ready workers for jobs that require a mix of abilities. This approach is especially gainful in powerful and quick moving workplaces.

In the time of remote work, nonconcurrent learning is acquiring conspicuousness. Nonconcurrent learning permits people to get to preparing materials at their own speed, autonomous of general setting. This adaptability is particularly invaluable for remote or geologically scattered groups, obliging various timetables and time regions. Nonconcurrent learning stages frequently incorporate recorded addresses, conversation discussions, and independent evaluations, giving a far reaching and open preparation experience.

Individual learning pathways engage people to take responsibility for proficient turn of events. As opposed to following a foreordained educational program, representatives can make customized learning plans in view of their vocation objectives and interests. This approach perceives that people have one of a kind yearnings and learning styles, permitting them to tailor their opportunities for growth as needs be. Individual learning pathways can consolidate a blend of formal preparation, independent review, and hands on learning valuable open doors.

Comprehensive plan standards are progressively affecting the improvement of preparing programs. Comprehensive plan expects to make opportunities for growth that are available to people with assorted capacities, foundations, and learning styles. This includes considering variables like language openness, clarity, and the utilization of interactive media to take special care of various learning inclinations. By taking on comprehensive plan rehearses, associations guarantee that their preparation drives are open and helpful to a different labor force.

Blockchain innovation is making advances into credentialing and confirmation processes. Blockchain's decentralized and secure nature takes into account the formation of evident advanced qualifications. This development tends to the test of certification misrepresentation and furnishes people with a compact and sealed record of their accomplishments. Blockchain-based accreditations can be handily imparted to bosses, instructive foundations, and different partners, smoothing out the check cycle.

The mix of information examination into labor force preparing programs is upgrading the capacity to gauge and assess the effect of learning drives. By gathering and examining information on student execution, commitment, and results, associations gain significant bits of knowledge into the adequacy of their preparation programs. Information investigation additionally empower constant improvement, permitting associations to emphasize on their preparation methodologies in view of continuous criticism and advancing business needs.

Turn around tutoring flips the customary mentorship model by matching more youthful, less experienced representatives with additional old pros. In this methodology, more youthful representatives, frequently alluded to as converse tutors, share their ability in regions like innovation, online entertainment, and arising patterns with their more experienced partners. This equal relationship encourages cross-generational learning and gives laid out experts experiences into the changing elements of the advanced work environment.

The gig economy has provoked a reconsideration of how preparing is drawn nearer for consultants and self employed entities. Consultants frequently search out preparing amazing open doors that are adaptable, centered, and straightforwardly pertinent to their flow or likely undertakings. Online stages that proposal on-request courses and certificates take care of the gig economy's requirement for deftness

5.3 Technology-Enabled Learning Platforms

In the contemporary scene of schooling and expert turn of events, innovation empowered learning stages have arisen as groundbreaking apparatuses, reshaping the manner in which people procure information and abilities. These stages influence advanced innovations to convey instructive substance in assorted designs, giving adaptability, availability, and intuitiveness. From customary scholastic subjects to particular expert preparation, innovation empowered learning stages have become vital to deep rooted learning and professional success.

One of the vital qualities of innovation empowered learning is the adaptability it offers. Students can get to content whenever, anyplace, breaking liberated from the imperatives of conventional homerooms and fixed plans. Nonconcurrent realizing, where members draw in with content at their own speed, has turned into a sign of numerous web-based stages. This adaptability is especially favorable for people with different responsibilities like everyday work, family obligations, or geological requirements.

The ascent of Monstrous Open Internet based Courses (MOOCs) represents the effect of innovation on schooling. MOOCs are online courses that take care of a gigantic worldwide crowd, permitting anybody with a web association with select. Stages like Coursera, edX, and Udacity offer courses from top colleges and organizations, covering a large number of subjects.

MOOCs democratize admittance to excellent training, empowering people all over the planet to improve their abilities and seek after mastering open doors that were once restricted to specific socioeconomics.

Versatile learning, controlled by man-made brainpower (simulated intelligence) and AI calculations, is one more feature of innovation empowered learning. These frameworks investigate students' presentation and designer the substance to their singular necessities, assets, and shortcomings. Versatile learning stages give a customized growth opportunity, guaranteeing that every student advances at an ideal speed and spotlights on regions that require extra consideration. This approach improves the productivity and viability of instructive intercessions.

Online degree programs presented by colleges and instructive organizations have acquired fame, furnishing people with the amazing chance to procure perceived capabilities through remote learning. These projects cover assorted fields, from business and innovation to humanities and medical care. The adaptability of online degrees requests to working experts looking to propel their professions without taking a break. Besides, online degrees frequently integrate intuitive components like virtual labs, conversation discussions, and cooperative tasks, reproducing a really captivating and vivid growth opportunity.

Virtual homerooms and online courses have become essential parts of innovation empowered learning. These stages work with constant connection among teachers and students, paying little mind to geological distances. Video conferencing instruments, like Zoom and Microsoft Groups, empower simultaneous correspondence, encouraging a feeling of local area among students. Virtual study halls are especially successful for conversations, back and forth discussions, and cooperative exercises, repeating a few parts of customary homeroom elements in a web-based climate.

The gamification of learning has added a component of commitment and inspiration to innovation empowered stages. Gamified components, like focuses, identifications, and lists of competitors, change learning into a more intuitive and serious experience. Gamification catches the consideration of students as well as boosts progress and accomplishment. This approach is particularly viable in making learning pleasant, especially for more youthful ages acquainted with gaming conditions.

Intelligent reproductions and computer generated reality (VR) innovations take experiential figuring out how higher than ever. Recreations duplicate true situations, permitting students to apply hypothetical information in useful circumstances. VR, with its vivid capacities, gives a reproduced climate where clients can communicate with three-layered content.

Enterprises like medical care, flight, and assembling influence VR to prepare experts in a gamble free and controlled setting. This active methodology upgrades maintenance and down to earth use of abilities.

Microlearning has acquired fame as a period effective and centered way to deal with learning. Innovation empowered stages convey content in scaled down modules, tending to explicit points or abilities. These short, designated illustrations oblige the advanced student's inclination for fast, open, and in a hurry learning. Microlearning is frequently used to give in the nick of time data, empowering students to secure information in little augmentations on a case by case basis.

The mix of computerized reasoning (computer based intelligence) and AI in learning stages stretches out past versatile learning. Artificial intelligence controlled chatbots and remote helpers offer prompt help and direction to students. These astute frameworks can answer inquiries, offer clarifications, and guide clients through learning ways. The constant input and help add to a more responsive and steady learning climate.

Blockchain innovation is making advances into the domain of credentialing and accreditation in training. Blockchain's decentralized and secure nature empowers the production of sealed advanced qualifications. Scholarly accomplishments, confirmations, and identifications can be put away on a blockchain, giving a straightforward and certain record of a singular's capabilities. This advancement tends to worries connected with certification extortion and improves on the confirmation cycle for businesses and instructive establishments.

Cooperative learning stages work with bunch based exercises and tasks, cultivating communication and information dividing between students. These stages frequently incorporate highlights like conversation gatherings, bunch tasks, and cooperative record altering. By making a virtual space for cooperation and correspondence, cooperative learning stages imitate the social parts of customary study halls, advancing a feeling of local area and aggregate critical thinking.

Customized learning pathways engage people to fit their instructive excursion as indicated by their objectives and inclinations. Innovation empowered stages permit students to look over different courses, modules, and assets in view of their inclinations and vocation desires. Customized learning pathways perceive that people have extraordinary learning styles and targets, advancing a more individualized and independent way to deal with instruction.

Nonconcurrent conversation discussions are normal highlights in numerous web based learning stages. These gatherings give a space to students to take part in conversations, seek clarification on pressing issues, and offer experiences with friends and educators.

The offbeat nature permits members to contribute whenever it might suit them, obliging different time regions and timetables. Conversation discussions work with cooperative advancing as well as make a feeling of local area among students.

Digital recordings and book recordings have become well known designs for conveying instructive substance. Innovation empowered stages perceive the worth of hear-able learning and give choices to people to consume data through verbally expressed word designs. Digital broadcasts and book recordings offer adaptability for in a hurry picking up, permitting people to pay attention to instructive substance during drives, exercises, or other day to day exercises.

Learning investigation, energized by information gathered from online stages, empower organizations and teachers to survey the adequacy of instructive mediations. These investigation give experiences into student commitment, progress, and regions that might need extra help. By utilizing information, teachers can refine their showing techniques, recognize patterns in student execution, and pursue informed choices to improve the general opportunity for growth.

Online entertainment stages assume a double part in innovation empowered learning. On one hand, stages like LinkedIn and Twitter act as spaces for proficient systems administration and information sharing. Then again, a few instructive organizations influence virtual entertainment highlights for cooperative advancing inside unambiguous courses. Online entertainment improves the feeling of local area among students, permitting them to interface past the limits of the learning stage.

Expanded reality (AR) supplements customary learning materials by overlaying advanced content onto the actual world. AR improves representations, rejuvenating unique ideas and giving intuitive encounters. In instructive settings, AR can be utilized for exercises like intelligent course books, virtual visits, and life systems models. The vivid idea of AR connects with students and improves how they might interpret complex subjects.

Open Instructive Assets (OER) are unreservedly available, straight-forwardly authorized materials that can be utilized for educating, learning, and exploration. Innovation empowered stages frequently integrate OER to give a savvy and open option in contrast to conventional course readings and assets. This approach upholds the guideline of open schooling, making top notch instructive materials accessible to a worldwide crowd without monetary boundaries.

Language learning stages influence innovation to offer intelligent and vivid encounters for procuring new dialects. These stages frequently use gamification, virtual conditions, and ongoing criticism to upgrade language obtaining.

Students can work on talking, tuning in, and perusing in a steady and dynamic web-based climate. Language learning stages take special care of a different crowd trying to gain or further develop language abilities for individual or expert reasons.

5.4 Corporate Responsibility in Employee Development

Corporate obligation in representative improvement has developed into a key part of hierarchical system, mirroring a promise to cultivating a talented, connected with, and versatile labor force. This responsibility stretches out past customary thoughts of representative preparation to include a more extensive vision of expert development, prosperity, and social obligation. As associations explore the intricacies of the cutting edge business scene, they perceive that putting resources into the improvement of their workers isn't simply an issue of consistence however an essential basic that adds to long haul achievement.

At the center of corporate obligation in worker improvement is the acknowledgment that representatives are a significant resource, and their development lines up with the association's objectives. This includes giving learning and improvement valuable open doors that go past fundamental work prerequisites, permitting representatives to gain abilities that add to their vocation movement and occupation fulfill-ment. By putting resources into the consistent learning and upskilling of workers, associations upgrade individual execution as well as reinforce their general capacities and intensity.

One vital component of corporate obligation in worker advancement is the arrangement of admittance to progressing preparing and instructive assets. This incorporates formal preparation programs, studios, online courses, and other learning drives that empower representatives to gain new abilities and keep up to date with industry patterns. Associations perceive that the business scene is dynamic, and representatives need to ceaselessly refresh their abilities to stay viable givers. By offering an assortment of learning valuable open doors, associations engage representatives to take responsibility for proficient turn of events.

Moreover, corporate obligation in representative improvement envelops a promise to making a strong learning society inside the association. This includes encouraging a climate where interest, trial and error, and persistent learning are esteemed. Associations can develop a learning society by advancing coordinated effort, giving time and assets to learning exercises, and perceiving and compensating representatives for their obligation to gaining new abilities. In such a climate, representatives feel urged to investigate groundbreaking thoughts, share information, and effectively take part in their own turn of events.

Mentorship programs assume a urgent part in corporate obligation, offering experienced experts the chance to guide and support less experienced associates. Mentorship cultivates a culture of information move, where the skill of prepared workers is imparted to the people who are prior in their vocations.

This not just adds to the advancement of individual abilities yet in addition fortifies the hierarchical information base. Mentorship programs show a guarantee to the development and outcome of representatives past their nearby work liabilities.

In the domain of corporate obligation, associations are progressively perceiving the significance of giving assets to representatives to seek after advanced education and postgraduate educations. Educational cost repayment projects and organizations with instructive foundations are instances of drives that help representatives in advancing their conventional training. This advantages individual vocation improvement as well as upgrades the association's scholarly capital by encouraging a labor force with cutting edge information and mastery.

Corporate obligation in worker improvement stretches out past expert abilities to envelop comprehensive prosperity. Perceiving the interconnection between physical, mental, and profound prosperity, associations are carrying out health programs that address different aspects of representatives' lives. These projects might incorporate wellness drives, psychological well-being support, stress the board assets, and balance between fun and serious activities drives. An emphasis on representative prosperity adds to a positive work environment culture and improves generally work fulfillment and efficiency.

Variety, value, and consideration (DEI) drives are fundamental to corporate obligation in worker improvement. Associations are perceiving the significance of establishing a comprehensive climate that values variety and gives equivalent open doors to all workers. DEI drives might include designated preparing programs, mentorship amazing open doors for underrepresented gatherings, and the foundation of comprehensive strategies and practices. By encouraging a different and comprehensive work environment, associations add to the expert improvement of all representatives and tap into a more extensive scope of viewpoints and gifts.

Corporate social obligation (CSR) incorporates drives that go past the inner improvement of workers to address more extensive cultural necessities. Associations are progressively mindful of their part in adding to the prosperity of the networks where they work. This might include putting resources into instructive projects in nearby networks, supporting professional preparation drives, or partaking in associations with non-benefit associations that attention on labor force advancement. Such drives line up with corporate obligation as well as add to a positive corporate picture and brand notoriety.

In the period of remote and mixture work models, corporate obligation in representative advancement incorporates contemplations for the extraordinary difficulties and valuable open doors introduced by these plans. Associations are putting resources into innovation and foundation to help remote picking up, furnishing workers with the instruments and assets required for powerful virtual cooperation and expert turn of events.

Furthermore, associations are aware of advancing a solid balance between fun and serious activities in distant conditions, stressing the significance of prosperity with regards to adaptable work plans.

Execution the executives frameworks that line up with corporate obligation in representative advancement center around consistent criticism, objective setting, and abilities appraisal. These frameworks go past customary yearly surveys to give progressing bits of knowledge into individual execution and development regions. By encouraging a culture of consistent criticism and acknowledgment, associations support workers in their improvement processes and make a powerful input circle that adjusts individual objectives to hierarchical targets.

Initiative improvement is a basic part of corporate obligation, perceiving that viable pioneers add to the general achievement and manageability of the association. Administration improvement projects might incorporate preparation, training, and mentorship drives pointed toward developing the up and coming age of pioneers. Associations are aware of the significance of different initiative groups that bring various points of view and encounters to dynamic cycles.

With regards to corporate obligation, associations are progressively embracing the idea of deep rooted learning. This includes recognizing that learning isn't restricted to explicit phases of one's profession however is a persistent and developing cycle. Associations that advance a culture of long lasting learning urge representatives to seek after learning valuable open doors all through their professions, adjusting to changing industry patterns and innovations. Deep rooted learning lines up with the possibility that people can obtain new abilities and rehash themselves at different phases of their expert process.

Representative commitment is a key measurement in evaluating the progress of corporate obligation in worker improvement. Drawn in representatives are bound to put resources into their own turn of events, contribute emphatically to the work environment culture, and adjust their objectives to those of the association. Associations that focus on representative commitment perceive the benefit of establishing a workplace where representatives feel esteemed, upheld, and persuaded to succeed. This includes cultivating open correspondence, giving open doors to proficient development, and perceiving and commending individual and aggregate accomplishments.

Straightforward correspondence is fundamental in corporate obligation, guaranteeing that workers are educated about accessible advancement amazing open doors, hierarchical objectives, and the more extensive effect of their commitments. Straightforward correspondence fabricates trust and encourages a feeling of arrangement among individual and hierarchical goals. By keeping workers informed, associations engage them to arrive at informed conclusions about their expert turn of events and effectively add to the accomplishment of hierarchical objectives.

Moral contemplations are essential to corporate obligation in representative turn of events. Associations should guarantee that preparing programs, mentorship drives, and execution the executives frameworks stick to moral standards and regard the pride and variety of workers. Moral contemplations additionally reach out to issues like information protection, fair treatment, and the aversion of segregation. By maintaining moral norms, associations show a promise to dependable strategic policies and add to a positive working environment culture.

The estimation and assessment of the effect of representative advancement drives are fundamental parts of corporate obligation. Associations utilize key execution pointers (KPIs) and measurements to evaluate the viability of preparing programs, track representative fulfillment, and measure the general effect on authoritative execution. This information driven approach permits associations to refine their procedures, dispense assets really, and guarantee that representative advancement drives line up with more extensive business goals.

8

Chapter 6

Socioeconomic Impact

The entwining web of financial variables assumes a crucial part in molding the direction of human social orders, impacting everything from individual prosperity to worldwide monetary scenes. As we explore the mind boggling woven artwork of contemporary presence, it turns out to be progressively apparent that the financial effect is extensive, addressing different features of existence with significant ramifications for the present and future.

At the core of this complicated transaction lies the idea of imbalance — an unavoidable power that shows itself in different structures, like pay difference, admittance to training, medical services, and valuable open doors. The repercussions of such incongruities are diverse, affecting the texture of social orders and deciding the existence directions of people. While analyzing financial effect, one can't get away from the inseparable connection between monetary frameworks and social designs.

The worldwide monetary request, set apart by industrialist standards, has been a predominant power molding the cutting edge world. Free enterprise, with its accentuation on confidential proprietorship, market-driven economies, and benefit thought process, has impelled remarkable monetary development yet has likewise been a harbinger of imbalance. The financial effect of free enterprise is obvious in the enlarging hole between the well-to-do and the underestimated, as abundance will in general gather in the possession of a couple, leaving huge segments of society on the edges of flourishing.

Pay imbalance, a sign of entrepreneur social orders, makes a progressive system that saturates different parts of life. It directs admittance to quality training, medical care, and valuable open doors for individual and expert development. The repercussions of such differences are frequently intergenerational, propagating patterns of neediness and restricting social portability. The gap between the wealthy and the poor turns into a favorable place for social distress, as disappointed networks wrestle with the obvious feeling of shamefulness.

Schooling, as a foundation of cultural advancement, embodies the financial effect in an unmistakable way. Differences in instructive access and quality enhance existing imbalances, as people from advantaged foundations approach better schools, assets, and open doors for scholastic progression. This makes a gap that reaches out into adulthood, influencing work possibilities and pay levels.

Also, the computerized partition fuels these instructive abberations. In a period overwhelmed by innovation, inconsistent admittance to computerized assets enlarges the hole between the people who can saddle the force of data and those left on the outskirts. The financial effect of this advanced separation is significant, as it influences instructive results as well as shapes the scene of work, development, and metro commitment.

Medical care, one more basic component of financial effect, mirrors the differences imbued in cultural designs. Admittance to quality medical care is much of the time dependent upon monetary status, with underestimated networks confronting obstructions to fundamental administrations. The repercussions are desperate, as wellbeing results become an impression of social honor. The Coronavirus pandemic, specifically, revealed the separation points in medical care frameworks around the world, highlighting the financial abberations in weakness and versatility.

The interchange between financial variables and medical care stretches out past individual prosperity to cultural versatility and general wellbeing. Minimized people group, troubled by financial difficulties, frequently wrestle with lacking medical care foundation, restricted admittance to preventive measures, and elevated weakness to pandemics. The recurrent idea of this relationship builds up the more extensive story of how financial differences shape the texture of social orders.

The work market, as a nexus of monetary and social powers, exemplifies the complicated dance among people and frameworks. Business, a foundation of financial soundness, isn't simply a method for occupation yet an impression of fundamental elements. The idea of work, portrayed by mechanical headways, globalization, and developing enterprises, adds to the reshaping of financial scenes.

Robotization, for example, has arisen as a blade that cuts both ways, promising productivity and development yet additionally representing a danger to conventional business. The financial effect of mechanization is unmistakable, with specific areas seeing position dislodging and a change in expertise prerequisites. This represents a test for people whose jobs are disturbed, requiring versatility and upskilling to explore the developing business scene.

Globalization, a characterizing element of the contemporary time, entwines economies and social orders in manners that rise above borders. While globalization has worked with the progression of merchandise, data, and capital, its effect on financial designs is nuanced. On one hand, it has opened roads for monetary development and innovative advancement; on the other, it has added to the enlarging hole among created and creating areas.

The financial effect of globalization is clear in the elements of exchange, speculation, and social trade. Creating economies, frequently consigned to fringe jobs in the worldwide monetary request, wrestle with difficulties like financial reliance, abuse of work, and natural debasement. The quest for monetary development, powered by globalization, some of the time comes at the expense of social value and natural manageability.

Ecological maintainability, a squeezing worry in the 21st 100 years, highlights the many-sided connection between financial frameworks and the planet. The abuse of regular assets, driven by free private enterprise and unrestrained utilization, has prompted natural uneven characters with extensive results. The financial effect of natural corruption isn't uniform and lopsidedly influences weak networks.

Environmental change, an outcome of impractical practices, worsens existing disparities. Minimized people group, frequently dwelling in naturally delicate regions, endure the worst part of environment related calamities and disturbances. The nexus between financial elements and natural maintainability is a call to rethink existing ideal models and take a stab at comprehensive and supportable turn of events.

The job of administration in molding financial results couldn't possibly be more significant. Political frameworks, strategies, and foundations use huge impact in deciding the dissemination of assets, open doors, and power inside a general public. Comprehensive and responsible administration can moderate the unfavorable impacts of financial variations, encouraging a more fair and just society.

Debasement, an unavoidable test in numerous social orders, enhances existing disparities by redirecting assets from fundamental administrations and public merchandise. The financial effect of debasement is significant, blocking monetary turn of events, dissolving trust in organizations, and sustaining patterns of neediness. Addressing debasement requires foundational changes and a pledge to straightforwardness and responsibility.

Social portability, the capacity of people to go up or down the financial stepping stool, fills in as a gauge of cultural wellbeing. In even-handed social orders, social versatility is a practical possibility, permitting people to rise above the conditions of their introduction to the world. In any case, when financial boundaries hinder up portability, social orders risk solidification, with dug in disparity turning into a characterizing highlight.

Mechanical progressions, while adding to financial development, additionally have suggestions for the financial texture. The computerized time has introduced uncommon network and advancement, yet it has additionally brought about new difficulties. The gig economy, set apart by brief and adaptable business, mirrors the changing idea of work. While it offers valuable open doors for business and adaptability, it additionally raises worries about professional stability, advantages, and laborers' privileges.

The financial effect of the gig economy stretches out past individual laborers to cultural designs. Conventional ideas of work, with stable positions and social security nets, are being reclassified. This shift requires a reconsideration of work regulations, social government assistance frameworks, and the actual idea of work in the 21st 100 years. As innovation keeps on reshaping businesses, the financial ramifications request cautious thought and proactive strategies.

The interconnection of financial elements becomes clear while looking at issues of orientation and race. Ladies, in spite of progress in numerous areas, keep on confronting variations in pay, portrayal, and admittance to open doors. The orientation pay hole, a determined test, reflects well established cultural standards and fundamental inclinations. Likewise, racial differences compound existing imbalances, with networks of variety confronting boundaries in schooling, business, and law enforcement.

The financial effect of fundamental bigotry and orientation imbalance is significant, profoundly shaping life results and building up verifiable treacheries. Multifaceted ways to deal with resolving these issues perceive the interconnected idea of different social personalities and take a stab at complete arrangements that destroy primary boundaries. Accomplishing genuine uniformity requires destroying the settled in frameworks that sustain separation and disservice.

Social union, the paste that ties different people into a working society, is naturally connected to financial elements. Comprehensive social orders that focus on civil rights and uniformity will quite often be stronger and firm. Alternately, social orders set apart by distinct abberations and avoidance risk discontinuity, with social agitation and dissension stewing underneath the surface.

6.1 Addressing Socioeconomic Disparities

Tending to financial incongruities requires an exhaustive and diverse methodology that traverses different spaces of society. From financial arrangements to training, medical care, and social frameworks, deliberate endeavors are expected to destroy the settled in structures that sustain disparity. The intricacies of financial inconsistencies request nuanced procedures that reduce quick difficulties as well as encourage long haul value and civil rights.

Financial changes stand at the front of tending to financial differences. A basic assessment of financial frameworks is basic, with an emphasis on strategies that advance comprehensive development and fair circulation of assets. Moderate tax assessment, for example, can assist with crossing over the abundance hole by guaranteeing that those with higher wages contribute proportionately more to help public administrations and social government assistance programs.

Moreover, designated mediations are important to elevate minimized networks that have generally confronted monetary avoidance. This incorporates drives, for example, governmental policy regarding minorities in society, local area advancement projects, and backing for little and minority-possessed organizations. Establishing an empowering climate for business venture inside these networks can spike financial strengthening and add to a more fair dissemination of riches.

Notwithstanding financial changes, instructive strategies assume a vital part in tending to financial variations. Training is a strong balancer, giving people the devices to beat boundaries and seek after potential open doors. Notwithstanding, foundational imbalances in admittance to quality training continue, sustaining patterns of weakness.

To address this, interests in training should focus on assets for underserved networks, guaranteeing that schools in financially impeded regions approach quality educators, offices, and instructive materials. Grants, awards, and mentorship projects can work with the passage of understudies from underestimated foundations into advanced education, separating boundaries to social portability.

Also, the computerized partition, which fuels instructive differences, should be connected. Admittance to innovation and the web is as of now not an extravagance however a need for scholastic achievement and expert development.

Drives that give reasonable or free web access, also as gadgets, can even the odds, guaranteeing that all understudies have equivalent chances to saddle the advantages of advanced learning.

Medical care, as a principal mainstay of cultural prosperity, requires designated techniques to address incongruities. General admittance to quality medical care is a basic freedom, yet numerous people, especially those in low-pay networks, face hindrances to fundamental administrations. Wellbeing variations in view of financial elements are apparent in regions like future, maternal and kid wellbeing, and the commonness of persistent illnesses.

To address these abberations, medical services frameworks should focus on preventive consideration, local area wellbeing drives, and effort programs in underserved regions. Reasonable and available medical care administrations, including immunizations, screenings, and essential consideration, can moderate the effect of financial elements on wellbeing results. Moreover, tending to the social determinants of wellbeing, like lodging, work, and training, is indispensable to making a comprehensive way to deal with prosperity.

The job of administration in forming financial results couldn't possibly be more significant. Straightforward, responsible, and comprehensive administration is fundamental for establishing a climate where strategies successfully address incongruities. Against defilement measures are essential to guarantee that assets are distributed evenhandedly and arrive at the people who need them the most.

Besides, policymaking ought to include the dynamic cooperation of different voices, including delegates from underestimated networks. Comprehensive dynamic cycles lead to strategies that are more receptive to the requirements of the whole populace, adding to a more pleasant and all the more society. A promise to basic liberties, uniformity, and civil rights ought to be implanted in the texture of administration structures at all levels.

Social security nets assume a critical part in moderating the effect of financial variations, giving a pad to people and families confronting monetary difficulties. Powerful friendly government assistance programs, including joblessness benefits, lodging help, and food security drives, can keep weak populaces from slipping further into neediness during seasons of monetary vulnerability.

In addition, tending to abberations in the law enforcement framework is fundamental to accomplishing civil rights. Racial and financial inclinations inside the law enforcement framework add to the propagation of imbalance. Changes that emphasis on local area policing, law enforcement training, and the recovery of wrongdoers can add to a more impartial and just framework.

In the domain of business, techniques that advance comprehensive monetary development are crucial. Work creation programs, professional preparation, and drives that help business in underestimated networks can add to breaking the pattern of neediness. Moreover, tending to wage holes and guaranteeing fair work rehearses are fundamental stages toward making an evenhanded labor force.

The confidential area likewise assumes a significant part in tending to financial differences. Companies can take on socially dependable strategic policies, including fair wages, variety and consideration drives, and local area commitment programs. Putting resources into nearby networks, especially in regions confronting financial difficulties, can add to economical turn of events and social upliftment.

Natural manageability is entwined with financial differences, as weak networks frequently endure the worst part of ecological debasement. Arrangements that focus on supportable turn of events, sustainable power, and preservation can add to both ecological wellbeing and the prosperity of underestimated populaces. Besides, drives that engage networks to take part in natural stewardship can make a cooperative connection among social and biological flexibility.

The worldwide local area has an aggregate liability to address worldwide financial differences. This includes giving guide to agricultural countries as well as resolving foundational issues, for example, unreasonable exchange rehearses, obligation loads, and the effect of globalization on weak economies. Cooperative endeavors to accomplish the Economical Improvement Objectives (SDGs) can act as an outline for worldwide fortitude and shared liability.

6.2 Policy Frameworks for a Balanced Automated Workforce

The fast headway of mechanization and man-made brainpower has introduced another period in the labor force scene, introducing the two open doors and difficulties. As innovation keeps on reshaping ventures, it is basic to foster strategy systems that figure out some kind of harmony between tackling the advantages of robotization and guaranteeing the prosperity of laborers. A proactive and complete methodology is expected to explore this change, one that tends to financial, social, and moral contemplations.

At the center of strategy structures for a fair robotized labor force is the acknowledgment that robotization can prompt expanded proficiency, development, and monetary development. In any case, these advantages should be combined with measures to relieve possible adverse consequences on business, pay imbalance, and cultural prosperity. Policymakers should be ground breaking, expecting the progressions achieved via mechanization and proactively forming the future universe of work.

One critical part of strategy structures is the reexamination of training and labor force advancement. The abilities expected in the mechanized labor force are developing quickly, and there is a developing requirement for a labor force that is versatile, mechanically proficient, and furnished with the abilities that supplement mechanization.

Training strategies should focus on STEM (science, innovation, designing, and math) schooling, computerized education, and deep rooted learning valuable chances to guarantee that people can flourish in an innovation driven economy.

In addition, arrangements ought to zero in on reskilling and up-skilling programs that empower laborers to change into new jobs and businesses. Putting resources into preparing programs for the on-going labor force, especially in areas powerless to computerization, can assist with relieving position relocation and encourage a stronger work market. Joint effort between instructive foundations, organizations, and government offices is fundamental to adjust preparing projects to the developing requests of the gig market.

Pair with labor force improvement, social wellbeing nets should be reinforced to give a cradle to laborers confronting uprooting because of robotization. Strategies ought to consider imaginative methodologies, for example, convenient advantages that are attached to people instead of explicit positions. This guarantees that specialists approach funda-mental advantages like medical care, retirement plans, and joblessness protection no matter what their work status, advancing monetary secu-rity in a time of expanded work portability.

Besides, the idea of an all inclusive fundamental pay (UBI) has built up forward momentum as a potential strategy reaction to the difficul-ties presented via mechanization. UBI includes giving a customary, un-restricted installment to all residents, paying little heed to work status. This approach intends to address pay imbalance, decrease destitution, and give a monetary security net to people whose positions might be uprooted via mechanization. Experimental runs projects and examina-tion on the practicality and effect of UBI ought to be considered to illuminate proof based policymaking in this space.

In the administrative domain, policymakers should figure out some kind of harmony between encouraging advancement and guaranteeing the moral utilization of computerization advances. Laying out clear rules for the dependable turn of events and arrangement of robotized frameworks is fundamental to forestall manhandles and safeguard the freedoms of laborers. This incorporates contemplations for algorithmic straightforwardness, responsibility, and the moral treatment of information, especially in ventures where mechanization assumes a critical part.

Work regulations likewise require cautious survey and transformation to the changing idea of work. Approaches ought to resolve issues, for example, gig work, independent game plans, and the freedoms of laborers in contemporary business connections. This incorporates looking at the order of laborers, guaranteeing fair wages, and stretching out work assurances to laborers in the gig economy. Policymakers should be proactive in expecting and addressing potential escape clauses that could leave laborers powerless against double-dealing in robotized workplaces.

Notwithstanding homegrown strategies, a worldwide viewpoint is pivotal while forming structures for a fair robotized labor force. The interconnected idea of the worldwide economy implies that the effects of robotization rise above public lines. Worldwide cooperation is crucial for share best practices, fit principles, and address difficulties, for example, the potential offshoring of occupations to nations with careless guidelines on robotization.

Besides, policymakers ought to think about the international ramifications of mechanization, remembering the potential for work uprooting for specific districts and the requirement for a worldwide reaction to address the subsequent monetary and social difficulties. Cooperative endeavors at the global level can likewise assist with forestalling a rush to the base regarding work guidelines and urge a rush to the top, where nations contend to lay out the most moral and laborer cordial strategies.

Moral contemplations are principal in the turn of events and sending of mechanization advances. Approaches ought to advance straightforwardness and responsibility in the utilization of calculations, guaranteeing that dynamic cycles are fair, impartial, and liberated from separation. Moral rules ought to be laid out to administer the utilization of computerization in delicate regions like medical services, law enforcement, and back to forestall unseen side-effects and guarantee the mindful utilization of innovation to assist society.

Besides, arrangements should address the moral ramifications of occupation relocation and the expected disintegration of human poise related with joblessness. Drives that empower the formation of significant work, even notwithstanding robotization, ought to be investigated. This might include supporting artistic expression, culture, and local area advancement projects that add to the prosperity of society past customary business measurements.

Public-private organizations are instrumental in molding a fair robotized labor force. Policymakers ought to draw in with industry partners to comprehend the particular difficulties and amazing open doors related with robotization in various areas. Cooperative endeavors can prompt the improvement of industry-explicit rules, best practices, and principles that line up with more extensive strategy goals.

Moreover, encouraging advancement environments that help the improvement of robotization advancements can situate nations and locales as pioneers in the worldwide market. Strategies that boost innovative work, business venture, and the reception of mechanization advances can add to monetary development while guaranteeing that the advantages are generally shared.

6.3 The Role of Governments in Managing Transition

Even with fast mechanical progressions and cultural changes, the job of state run administrations in overseeing advances has become progressively basic. The dynamism of the contemporary scene, set apart by elements like robotization, man-made reasoning, and globalization, requires proactive and vital administration to explore the difficulties and saddle the open doors introduced by these changes.

Training remains as a key part in overseeing changes, and states assume a crucial part in forming instructive strategies that outfit people with the abilities expected in the developing position market. By cultivating an educational program that underlines science, innovation, designing, and math (STEM) instruction, states can guarantee that the labor force is sufficiently ready for the requests of an innovatively driven economy. Moreover, drives advancing computerized proficiency and coding abilities are urgent to overcome any issues between the ongoing school system and the requirements of an undeniably digitized labor force.

Moreover, state run administrations should advocate drives zeroed in on reskilling and upskilling projects to enable existing laborers to adjust to changing position prerequisites. The thought of deep rooted learning is vital, and strategies ought to energize a culture of ceaseless expertise improvement, empowering people to stay nimble notwithstanding developing mechanical scenes. Cooperation between states, instructive establishments, and enterprises is fundamental to adjust preparing projects to the unique requests of the gig market.

Social wellbeing nets structure a basic part of overseeing changes, especially in the midst of monetary vulnerability and occupation uprooting. States ought to reinforce these wellbeing nets to offer a powerful help framework for people confronting joblessness or underemployment because of innovative movements. Convenient advantages that rise above unambiguous positions and follow people all through their vocations can offer a wellbeing net in a gig economy set apart by expanded work versatility.

The idea of a widespread fundamental pay (UBI) has gathered consideration as a likely instrument for overseeing changes. By giving a normal, unrestricted pay to all residents, independent of work status, UBI intends to address pay disparity, lessen neediness, and proposition monetary security to those whose positions might be dislodged via mechanization. Experimental runs programs and thorough exploration on the achievability and effect of UBI can direct proof based policymaking in this space.

In the administrative space, legislatures assume a pivotal part in molding the moral utilization of mechanization advancements. Clear rules are basic to guarantee mindful turn of events and sending, forestalling mishandles and shielding the privileges of laborers. Policymakers should focus on issues like algorithmic straightforwardness, responsibility, and the moral treatment of information, especially in businesses where robotization is pervasive.

Finding some kind of harmony between cultivating advancement and moral contemplations requires a lithe and versatile administrative system.

Work regulations request recalibration to line up with the developing idea of work. Policymakers should survey and adjust existing work regulations to resolve issues emerging from gig work, independent game plans, and the privileges of laborers in contemporary business connections. The grouping of laborers, fair wages, and the expansion of work securities to those in the gig economy require cautious thought to forestall double-dealing and guarantee a fair and impartial workplace.

Notwithstanding homegrown contemplations, legislatures should embrace a worldwide viewpoint in overseeing changes. The interconnected idea of the worldwide economy suggests that the effects of innovative movements rise above public boundaries. Worldwide cooperation becomes vital for share best practices, blend guidelines, and address difficulties, for example, the potential offshoring of occupations to nations with remiss guidelines on robotization. Cooperative endeavors at the worldwide level can assist with forestalling a rush to the base concerning work norms and urge a rush to the top, advancing moral and laborer cordial strategies internationally.

International ramifications additionally request consideration. Legislatures should expect and address potential work removal in specific districts, recognizing the requirement for an organized worldwide reaction to monetary and social difficulties coming about because of robotization. By cultivating worldwide participation and shared liability, states can explore the intricacies of worldwide changes and add to an additional evenhanded and maintainable future.

The moral contemplations inborn in the organization of computerization advancements require a proactive position from states. Policymakers should lay out clear rules that advance straightforwardness, responsibility, and reasonableness in the utilization of calculations. Moral contemplations stretch out to regions like medical services, law enforcement, and money, where the effect of computerization can be significant. Policymakers should guarantee that innovative headways line up with cultural qualities and add to everyone's benefit.

Public-private organizations arise as instrumental components in overseeing advances actually. State run administrations ought to effectively draw in with industry partners to comprehend the difficulties and open doors related with robotization in various areas. Cooperative endeavors can prompt the advancement of industry-explicit rules, best practices, and principles that line up with more extensive approach targets. Cultivating advancement biological systems through organizations can situate countries as pioneers in the worldwide market while guaranteeing that the advantages of robotization are broadly shared.

All in all, the job of states in overseeing changes is multi-layered, enveloping schooling, social security nets, guideline, and global coordinated effort. As the world wrestles with the extraordinary effects of mechanization, legislatures should be proactive in forming strategies that balance the advantages of mechanical headways with the prosperity of people and society at large. By supporting long lasting learning, moral contemplations, and worldwide collaboration, legislatures can explore the intricacies of changes and prepare for a future where the advantages of robotization are bridled capably and evenhandedly.

6.4 Socioeconomic Implications of Remote Work

The coming of remote work has introduced a change in outlook in the customary work environment elements, leading to a large group of financial ramifications that resound across different features of society. As innovation works with the decentralization of work, changing family rooms into workplaces and virtual gatherings into the new standard, the significant effects on people, organizations, and networks come into center. Looking at the financial ramifications of remote work divulges a perplexing embroidery that interweaves issues of balance between fun and serious activities, monetary imbalance, metropolitan country elements, and the eventual fate of work itself.

One of the striking impacts of remote work is the change of balance between serious and fun activities. By all accounts, the capacity to work remotely guarantees adaptability and independence, permitting people to fit their work hours to all the more likely line up with individual responsibilities and needs. This recently discovered adaptability, nonetheless, accompanies an expected disadvantage. The limit among expert and individual life becomes permeable, prompting difficulties in depicting work hours from individual time. The assumption for being continually accessible, combined with the obscuring of spatial limits between the home and the working environment, may add to a feeling of burnout and expanded feelings of anxiety among telecommuters.

In addition, the effect of remote work reaches out past the person to the nuclear family. With additional people telecommuting, there is an expected change in relational peculiarities as shared spaces become multifunctional, obliging both work and homegrown exercises. The renegotiation of family obligations and the requirement for clear correspondence inside families become pivotal elements together as one and prosperity.

Financial imbalance is one more aspect of the remote work scene that requires cautious thought. While remote work offers amazing open doors for experts in information based ventures to keep up with efficiency from anyplace with a web association, it might worsen existing abberations for those in positions that require actual presence, like assistance and assembling areas. This polarity can extend monetary imbalances, excessively affecting specific socioeconomics and compounding previous pay holes.

Moreover, the capacity to work remotely is dependent upon elements, for example, admittance to rapid web, a favorable home climate, and the idea of one's occupation. People in rustic or underserved regions might confront difficulties in getting to the essential framework for remote work, further compounding the metropolitan provincial separation. Policymakers need to address these differences to guarantee that remote work valuable open doors are open to a wide and various range of the labor force.

The metropolitan country elements, specifically, are going through a change because of the ascent of remote work. By and large, metropolitan focuses have been magnets for open positions, drawing people looking for business, social conveniences, and a lively public activity. The capacity to work from a distance, in any case, challenges the conventional thought of the metropolitan work center. As people never again need to dwell in vicinity to their working environment, there is potential for a reallocation of the labor force towards rural or provincial regions.

This shift has suggestions for both metropolitan and provincial networks. Metropolitan regions might encounter a decrease in populace thickness, influencing neighborhood organizations and framework intended to help a thick labor force. On the other side, rustic regions stand to profit from a deluge of telecommuters, possibly renewing nearby economies. Be that as it may, this likewise requires interests in advanced framework, medical care, and instructive assets to oblige the changing segment designs.

The ramifications of remote work stretch out to the eventual fate of work itself. As associations adjust to a remote or crossover work model, the conventional office space goes through a reconsideration. The interest for office land might diminish, affecting the business land area and the related enterprises that depend on office-driven plans of action. This shift difficulties regular ideas of corporate culture, cooperation, and advancement, provoking associations to reevaluate how they cultivate joint effort and union among remote groups.

The gig economy, portrayed by brief and adaptable business, converges with the remote work pattern. Remote work gives open doors to consultants and gig laborers to get to a more extensive scope of open positions, untethered by geological limitations. In any case, it likewise presents difficulties, for example, work uncertainty, absence of business benefits, and the potential for double-dealing. Policymakers need to address these difficulties to guarantee that the advantages of remote work are shared fairly across different business models.

Besides, the ramifications of remote work are not uniform across businesses. While innovation and information based areas consistently progress to remote work, businesses like assembling, medical services, and retail face extraordinary difficulties. Occupations requiring actual presence, involved errands, or direct client communications might find it trying to embrace remote work models.

Policymakers and organizations should cautiously consider the business explicit subtleties in creating arrangements that advance inclusivity and address the different requirements of the labor force.

The emotional wellness ramifications of remote work likewise warrant consideration. While remote work dispenses with driving and offers adaptability, it can add to sensations of seclusion and an absence of social association. The shortfall of eye to eye connections might affect group union and thwart the natural trade of thoughts that frequently happens in an actual working environment. Finding some kind of harmony between remote work and open doors for in-person joint effort becomes urgent for keeping up with both mental prosperity and expert development.

Network protection arises as a basic worry in the remote work scene. As people access delicate organization information from different areas, the gamble of online protection breaks increments. Policymakers and associations should focus on vigorous network safety measures to shield delicate data, safeguard against information breaks, and guarantee the security of telecommuters. Clear rules and guidelines are fundamental to lay out a solid structure for remote work without compromising information trustworthiness.

As the investigation of the financial ramifications of remote work digs further, it is significant to examine the perplexing snare of elements that shape the encounters of people, organizations, and social orders. One huge aspect is the effect of remote work on variety, value, and incorporation. While remote work can possibly separate geological hindrances and advance inclusivity, it likewise presents difficulties in keeping a feeling of having a place and equivalent open doors for all.

Variety in the labor force, enveloping perspectives like orientation, race, identity, and financial foundation, is a foundation of flourishing associations. Remote work, by rising above geological limitations, can add to a more different labor force as organizations tap into ability pools that were beforehand difficult to reach. Be that as it may, the potential for accidental predisposition in remote recruiting processes and the requirement for deliberate endeavors to encourage a comprehensive virtual workplace require cautious thought.

The idea of remote work likewise meets with orientation elements. On one hand, remote work can enable ladies by giving adaptability to adjust proficient and providing care liabilities. Then again, there is a gamble of compounding existing orientation imbalances, as remote work might escalate the weight of neglected providing care excessively bore by ladies. Policymakers and associations should be sensitive to these subtleties, making strategies that advance orientation value and make a steady structure for all kinds of people in the remote work scene.

In addition, the availability of remote work isn't uniform across financial layers. People with admittance to a devoted work space, high velocity web, and ergonomic work areas might encounter remote work more well than those without these assets. The financial differences in admittance to remote work foundation highlight the significance of designated mediations to connect the advanced separation and guarantee evenhanded open doors for all.

Little and medium-sized undertakings (SMEs) address a huge part of the worldwide economy. The ramifications of remote work for these organizations are nuanced, as they might come up short on assets and foundation of bigger partnerships. While remote work offers cost-saving open doors, it might likewise introduce difficulties as far as keeping up with group union, coordinated effort, and offering the vital help for representatives. Policymakers ought to fit their help measures to address the remarkable necessities of SMEs, perceiving their job as motors of financial development and work.

The drawn out ramifications of remote work on advancement and inventiveness inside associations merit careful investigation. While remote work can encourage individual independence and profound work, the unconstrained trade of thoughts that frequently happens in an actual work area might be reduced. The test for associations lies in developing a virtual climate that supports advancement, cooperation, and the cross-fertilization of thoughts. Strategies and practices that find some kind of harmony among independence and cooperative imagination are fundamental for associations planning to flourish in the period of remote work.

The convergence of remote work and psychological wellness has acquired conspicuousness as the limits among expert and individual life obscure. While remote work disposes of the pressure of driving, it acquaints new difficulties related with seclusion, forlornness, and the consistent computerized network that might add to burnout. Policymakers and associations need to focus on emotional wellness drives, offering assets, backing, and components to cultivate social association and balance between serious and fun activities in the remote work setting.

The job of authority in overseeing remote groups becomes urgent in guaranteeing hierarchical achievement. The customary authority model, based on actual presence and direct management, may require variation in the remote work scene. Pioneers need to develop trust, set clear assumptions, and carry out successful correspondence procedures to explore the difficulties of far off administration. Preparing projects and backing instruments for pioneers can work with this progress and encourage a culture of responsibility and joint effort.

Also, the ramifications of remote work stretch out to the actual framework of urban communities and metropolitan preparation. As remote work turns out to be more common, the interest for business office spaces might diminish, prompting likely changes in metropolitan scenes.

Metropolitan organizers and policymakers should expect these progressions and investigate versatile systems to reuse office spaces, advance blended use improvement, and guarantee supportable metropolitan conditions that line up with the developing idea of work.

The development of remote work likewise prompts a reexamination of transportation and driving examples. In the event that a critical piece of the labor force keeps on working from a distance, the interest for conventional methods of transportation, for example, day to day drives and business travel, may diminish. Policymakers ought to think about the ecological ramifications of these movements and investigate practical transportation options that line up with the changing elements of work.

The worldwide idea of remote work acquaints contemplations related with time regions, social contrasts, and global work regulations. Remote groups frequently range different geographic areas, expecting associations to explore difficulties in organizing work hours, obliging assorted social standards, and guaranteeing consistence with different lawful structures. Policymakers can contribute by cultivating worldwide joint efforts, blending work principles, and giving rules to associations to explore the intricacies of dealing with a worldwide distant labor force.

The ramifications of remote work for the business land area are significant. The shift toward remote work difficulties the customary interest for office spaces, possibly prompting an overflow of business land. Policymakers and metropolitan organizers need to imagine versatile techniques for reusing these spaces, taking into account factors, for example, reasonable lodging, public venues, or offices that help nearby business. This reconsidering of metropolitan spaces lines up with the more extensive objective of making tough and energetic networks.

In investigating the financial ramifications of remote work, the gig economy arises as a fundamental part of the conversation. Remote work and gig work share specific qualities, like adaptability and independence. People took part in gig work, frequently portrayed by present moment or task based commitment, may find arrangement with the remote work model. Policymakers should consider the convergences and qualifications between remote work and gig work, guaranteeing that strategies address the one of a kind necessities and difficulties of the two models to establish a strong and comprehensive workplace.

The lawful and administrative systems administering remote work likewise require investigation. Clear rules are vital for portray the expectations of the two businesses and representatives in the remote work scene. This incorporates contemplations connected with working hours, extra time pay, information security, and word related wellbeing and security. Policymakers ought to team up with worker's organizations, organizations, and legitimate specialists to make strong and versatile administrative structures that protect the interests, everything being equal.

9

Chapter 7

The Future Work Ecosystem

The future work biological system is going through a significant change, driven by mechanical progressions, moving cultural qualities, and the developing idea of ventures. As we explore the perplexing scene of work in the years to come, a few key patterns are molding the future workplace.

One of the most unmistakable movements is the ascent of remote work. The Coronavirus pandemic sped up the reception of remote work, and numerous associations have embraced it as a drawn out methodology. This progress has been worked with by headways in correspondence innovation, joint effort devices, and a developing accentuation on balance between fun and serious activities. Thus, the customary office-driven model is giving way to a more adaptable and decentralized approach.

Remote work achieves the two difficulties and open doors. On one hand, it permits associations to take advantage of a worldwide ability pool, encouraging variety and inclusivity. Then again, it requires new administration methodologies to guarantee efficiency, keep up with group attachment, and address issues connected with disengagement and burnout. The future work environment should find some kind of harmony between the advantages of remote work and the requirement for social association and joint effort.

Mechanization and computerized reasoning (artificial intelligence) are reshaping the idea of work by expanding human abilities and robotizing routine undertakings. Occupations that include monotonous and unsurprising undertakings are progressively being mechanized, while request is ascending for abilities that supplement computer based intelligence, like decisive reasoning, innovativeness, and the capacity to understand people at their core. The future labor force will probably be portrayed by a more popularity for abilities that are interestingly human.

Nonstop learning and upskilling will be fundamental to flourish in this advancing scene. Deep rooted learning programs, both formal and casual, will become vital to individual and expert turn of events. Associations should put resources into preparing and improvement drives to guarantee that their representatives stay significant in an always changing position market.

The gig economy is another pattern molding the future work environment. Outsourcing, free contracting, and gig work have become more common as people look for more noteworthy adaptability in their vocations. Stages that associate consultants with managers are on the ascent, setting out new open doors for the two laborers and organizations. Notwithstanding, the gig economy likewise brings up issues about employer stability, benefits, and the social wellbeing net, provoking a reconsideration of work strategies and guidelines.

Variety, value, and consideration (DEI) are acquiring expanded consideration later on work environment. Associations are perceiving the significance of building different and comprehensive groups, as an issue of social obligation as well as an upper hand. A different labor force brings alternate points of view, thoughts, and approaches, encouraging development and better direction. Organizations that focus on DEI drives will be better situated to draw in top ability and adjust to the changing socioeconomics of the worldwide labor force.

The fate of work is additionally interwoven with the idea of direction driven associations. Representatives today, particularly the more youthful age, are looking for something other than a check; they need to work for organizations that line up with their qualities and add to a more noteworthy cultural reason. Associations that focus on friendly and ecological obligation are bound to draw in and hold top ability, as well as serious areas of strength for fabricate with clients and partners.

The job of administration is advancing later on work biological system. Pioneers should explore the intricacies of a scattered and different labor force, encourage a culture of persistent learning, and embrace deft and versatile administration rehearses. The customary various leveled model might give way to more cooperative and comprehensive administration styles that engage workers and support advancement.

The actual work area is going through a change too. While remote work is turning out to be more pervasive, the workplace isn't vanishing altogether. All things being equal, it is developing into a space that underscores cooperation, imagination, and social communication. The workplace representing things to come might be planned as a center for group building, conceptualizing, and organizing, with adaptable workstations that oblige both face to face and remote work.

The future work biological system isn't without its difficulties. Protection concerns, information security, and the moral ramifications of man-made intelligence and robotization are regions that require cautious thought. As innovation keeps on propelling, there is a requirement for vigorous strategies and guidelines to guarantee that the advantages of development are offset with moral contemplations and the prosperity of laborers.

Wellbeing and prosperity will be at the very front of working environment needs. The occasions of the previous year have featured the significance of supporting representatives' psychological and actual wellbeing. Businesses are perceiving the need to establish a strong workplace that tends to pressure, burnout, and balance between serious and fun activities. Adaptable work courses of action, wellbeing programs, and psychological well-being assets will be basic parts representing things to come work environment.

Globalization will keep on molding the fate of work, with associations working in an undeniably interconnected and reliant world. Multifaceted joint effort, virtual groups, and worldwide ability portability will be fundamental for organizations to stay serious. The capacity to explore social contrasts and work successfully in a worldwide setting will be a significant expertise for the labor force representing things to come.

All in all, the future work environment is a dynamic and developing scene formed by mechanical, social, and financial powers. Remote work, robotization, the gig economy, variety and consideration, reason driven associations, developing administration models, and the rethinking of actual work areas are adding to a change in outlook by they way we approach work.

As we embrace these changes, it is pivotal to focus on the prosperity of people, encourage a culture of persistent learning, and guarantee that the advantages of development are shared impartially. The eventual fate of work is definitely not a foreordained objective yet an excursion that requires flexibility, imagination, and a pledge to building a feasible and comprehensive workplace. By exploring these difficulties and potential open doors nicely, we can shape a future work environment that benefits people, associations, and society overall.

7.1 Embracing the Automated Future

The fast progression of innovation, especially in the domains of robotization and man-made consciousness (man-made intelligence), is introducing another time that vows to alter the manner in which we work and live. As we stand on the cusp of this robotized future, there is a squeezing need to comprehend, adjust to, and embrace the extraordinary potential that these innovations bring.

Robotization, the utilization of machines or frameworks to perform errands without human intercession, has been a characterizing element of modern advancement. Nonetheless, late advancements in simulated intelligence and AI have raised mechanization higher than ever, empowering machines not exclusively to perform routine actual errands yet additionally to deal with mental undertakings that generally required human knowledge. This shift is reshaping businesses, work jobs, and the actual idea of work itself.

One of the essential regions affected via computerization is the labor force. Standard, dull assignments in assembling, information section, and client assistance are progressively being computerized, prompting expanded proficiency and cost-adequacy. While this can prompt work relocation in specific areas, it additionally opens up open doors for the labor force to take part in additional significant and complex undertakings that influence extraordinarily human abilities, like imagination, decisive reasoning, and the capacity to understand people on a deeper level.

The ascent of mechanization isn't restricted to actual assignments. Artificial intelligence calculations are becoming capable at breaking down huge measures of information, distinguishing examples, and making expectations. This has suggestions for dynamic cycles across different enterprises, from money to medical care. While the mix of artificial intelligence into independent direction can upgrade productivity and exactness, it additionally raises moral contemplations with respect to predisposition, straightforwardness, and responsibility.

In the domain of business, mechanization is changing authoritative designs and functional models. Organizations are progressively embracing mechanical cycle mechanization (RPA) to smooth out dull assignments, lessen blunders, and upgrade generally efficiency. This shift permits representatives to zero in on undertakings that require human judgment, imagination, and relational abilities. The outcome is a more deft and versatile labor force fit for answering unique market requests.

The mechanized future reaches out past individual associations to whole enterprises. The idea of "Industry 4.0" addresses the combination of robotization, information trade, and savvy advancements in assembling. This change in outlook is described by the Web of Things (IoT), digital actual frameworks, and distributed computing, making interconnected biological systems that upgrade creation processes and work with ongoing navigation.

While Industry 4.0 offers phenomenal effectiveness gains, it likewise requires a labor force with computerized proficiency and versatility.

In the medical care area, mechanization is upgrading analytic abilities, therapy arranging, and, surprisingly, surgeries. Simulated intelligence calculations can examine clinical pictures, identify examples, and help medical services experts in making more precise determinations. Mechanical medical procedure frameworks, directed by simulated intelligence, are progressively being utilized to carry out multifaceted strategies with accuracy, diminishing the wiggle room and working on persistent results.

While the advantages of mechanization are obvious, there are worries about its effect on work. The anxiety toward far reaching position dislodging has incited conversations about the requirement for reskilling and upskilling drives to set up the labor force for the positions representing things to come. As specific undertakings become mechanized, new jobs arise that require an alternate arrangement of abilities. Deep rooted learning and flexibility are becoming pivotal parts of profession improvement in the robotized time.

Also, the moral contemplations encompassing mechanization can't be overlooked. Inquiries concerning the moral utilization of computer based intelligence, information protection, and the potential for algorithmic inclination request cautious examination. As machines take on dynamic jobs, there is a requirement for straightforwardness in the calculations utilized and systems to address potentially negative side-effects. Finding some kind of harmony between mechanical headway and moral contemplations is basic for an amicable concurrence with robotization.

The robotized future likewise achieves changes in the idea of business venture. New companies are utilizing robotization and simulated intelligence to foster imaginative arrangements and disturb customary ventures. From computer based intelligence controlled chatbots for client support to independent vehicles reforming transportation, business visionaries are at the bleeding edge of making esteem through mechanization. Notwithstanding, they additionally face difficulties connected with administrative systems, moral rules, and public discernment.

The worldwide scene is seeing international ramifications of the mechanized future. Countries are competing for administration in simulated intelligence examination, advancement, and execution. The competition to foster simulated intelligence innovations that dominate contenders has turned into a point of convergence of monetary and key interests. Policymakers are wrestling with the need to encourage advancement while addressing concerns connected with work removal, moral principles, and public safety.

As we embrace the mechanized future, schooling assumes a vital part in setting up the labor force for the difficulties and valuable open doors ahead. Instructive foundations should adjust their educational plans to incorporate advanced proficiency, artificial intelligence essentials, and

decisive reasoning abilities. The objective is to furnish understudies with the information and capacities expected to flourish in our current reality where mechanization is vital to different parts of life.

The change to a mechanized future isn't without its cultural ramifications. The idea of widespread essential pay (UBI) has gotten some decent forward momentum as a likely answer for address the monetary incongruities coming about because of occupation uprooting. UBI proposes giving all residents an ordinary, genuine amount of cash, independent of business status, to meet their fundamental necessities. This thought intends to guarantee that the advantages of robotization are shared all the more evenhandedly across society.

In the domain of transportation, the computerized future is insepa-rable from the turn of events and arrangement of independent vehicles. The car business is seeing a change in outlook with the reconciliation of computer based intelligence, sensors, and network in vehicles. While independent vehicles hold the commitment of diminishing mishaps, further developing traffic stream, and improving availability, they addi-tionally raise moral quandaries, administrative difficulties, and worries about work dislodging in the transportation area.

Natural manageability is one more aspect of the mechanized future. Shrewd urban communities, empowered via robotization and IoT in-novations, expect to improve asset use, decrease energy utilization, and upgrade in general productivity. From brilliant lattices to savvy squan-der the executives frameworks, mechanization adds to building eco-accommodating metropolitan conditions. Nonetheless, accomplishing maintainability objectives requires a comprehensive methodology that thinks about the natural effect of assembling and discarding mechanized innovations.

In the domain of client care, chatbots and menial helpers fueled by simulated intelligence are becoming pervasive. These mechanized frameworks offer quick reactions, every minute of every day acces-sibility, and customized communications. While they upgrade client encounters and smooth out help processes, they additionally bring up issues about work relocation and the requirement for human touch in client connections.

Media outlets isn't insusceptible to the effect of robotization. Man-made intelligence calculations are utilized to investigate client inclina-tions and suggest content, forming the manner in which we consume media. Mechanization in satisfied creation, for example, the utilization of artificial intelligence produced music and fine art, challenges custom-ary thoughts of imagination and brings up issues about the job of human specialists in a computerized innovative scene.

Security concerns pose a potential threat in the robotized future. The interconnected idea of robotized frameworks conveys them vulnerable to digital intimidations and assaults. Defending basic foundation, delicate information, and man-made intelligence calculations from noxious entertainers is vital.

As robotization becomes fundamental to areas like money, medical services, and transportation, guaranteeing the versatility of these frameworks against digital dangers turns into a perplexing test that requires cooperation between legislatures, ventures, and online protection specialists.

The lawful scene is likewise advancing because of the mechanized future. As artificial intelligence frameworks pursue choices with lawful outcomes, inquiries concerning risk, responsibility, and straightforwardness come to the very front. Laying out legitimate structures that administer the utilization of man-made intelligence, safeguard individual freedoms, and guarantee moral guidelines is quite difficult for legislators all over the planet.

7.2 Building Sustainable and Adaptable Careers

In the always developing scene of work and vocations, the quest for manageability and flexibility has become progressively pivotal. As the elements of enterprises, advancements, and cultural assumptions keep on moving, people are constrained to fabricate professions that endure change as well as flourish in it. This requires a comprehensive methodology that envelops persistent learning, strength, and a promise to individual and expert development.

Maintainability with regards to vocations goes past the conventional comprehension of ecological obligation. It stretches out to the strength and significance of one's abilities and mastery even with mechanical progressions and financial changes. Building a manageable vocation includes a continuous course of securing new abilities, keeping up to date with industry drifts, and developing an outlook of versatility.

Persistent learning is at the center of feasible professions. In our current reality where innovation develops quickly, enterprises go through perspective changes, and new ranges of abilities arise, the capacity to learn and adjust turns into an essential resource. Deep rooted learning isn't simply a trendy expression however a need. It includes the proactive quest for information, whether through proper schooling, online courses, studios, or independent learning. The hug of a development outlook, where difficulties are seen as any open doors for learning and improvement, turns into a core value.

The coming of computerized stages and online instruction has democratized admittance to learning assets. People can now participate in expertise building exercises from the solace of their homes, considering more noteworthy adaptability in coordinating learning into their lives. This change in the learning scene empowers experts to upskill or reskill, taking care of the advancing requests of the gig market.

Mentorship and systems administration assume vital parts in supporting and propelling vocations. Tutors give direction, share encounters, and deal important experiences that can assist people with exploring the intricacies of their particular businesses. Organizing, both face to face and through advanced stages, works with the trading of thoughts, amazing open doors, and emotionally supportive networks.

Building a hearty expert organization upgrades one's capacity to remain informed about industry patterns, access open positions, and look for exhortation from old pros.

Versatility, firmly connected with supportability, is a vital characteristic for flourishing in a unique workplace. The capacity to turn, embrace change, and proactively look for open doors even with vulnerability positions people for long haul achievement. Flexibility includes not just the specialized abilities pertinent to a specific work yet additionally the delicate abilities that empower powerful correspondence, coordinated effort, and critical thinking.

The gig economy, portrayed by present moment and independent commitment, epitomizes the flexibility requested by the contemporary work market. Experts are progressively embracing gig fill in for the purpose of differentiating their abilities, acquiring changed encounters, and partaking in the adaptability it bears. In any case, the gig economy additionally presents difficulties, like pay unsteadiness, absence of advantages, and the requirement for self-advancement. Adjusting the advantages and difficulties of gig work requires an essential way to deal with vocation the executives.

Chasing manageable and versatile vocations, people should accept responsibility for proficient turn of events. This includes laying out clear objectives, surveying current abilities and capabilities, and distinguishing regions for development. The improvement of a customized profession plan, including present moment and long haul goals, gives a guide to exploring the intricacies of the gig market.

Vocation strength is intently attached to manageability and versatility. Strength includes the capacity to quickly return from misfortunes, explore through difficulties, and keep an inspirational perspective in the midst of vulnerabilities. Building strength requires developing areas of strength for an of self-viability, creating methods for dealing with especially difficult times for pressure, and cultivating a proactive mentality toward mishaps. Versatile people view difficulties as any open doors for development and influence affliction to reinforce their abilities and character.

Embracing a multidisciplinary way to deal with expertise improvement upgrades profession flexibility. The reconciliation of abilities from different spaces empowers experts to turn among jobs and ventures, answering successfully to changing business sector requests. T-molded experts, who have both profound mastery in a particular region and a wide scope of correlative abilities, are strategically set up to explore the developing position market.

Enterprising abilities are progressively esteemed with regards to feasible professions. The capacity to recognize amazing open doors, go ahead with reasonable courses of action, and improve isn't restricted to customary business visionaries. Business endeavor, or the utilization of enterprising abilities inside a hierarchical setting, is turning into a sought-after skill.

People who can drive advancement, explore uncertainty, and add to the development of their associations are profoundly esteemed in unique enterprises.

The idea of a "portfolio profession" embodies the flexibility and manageability expected in current vocations. Rather than depending on a solitary work or calling, people with portfolio professions take part in a blend of jobs, tasks, and exercises that influence their different abilities and interests. This approach gives versatility against financial vulnerabilities and considers more noteworthy adaptability in answering advancing vocation goals.

Maintainable and versatile professions likewise request a proactive way to deal with individual marking. In a carefully associated world, people are assessed in view of their list of qualifications as well as on their web-based presence. Building major areas of strength for a brand includes exhibiting one's skill, values, and remarkable characteristics through proficient profiles, web-based entertainment, and online portfolios. A very much created individual brand draws in open doors as well as lays out believability according to friends, managers, and teammates.

The crossing point of innovation and professions presents the idea of computerized education as a fundamental expertise. Advanced proficiency goes past the capacity to utilize computerized apparatuses; it envelops decisive contemplating data, moral contemplations in advanced cooperations, and the ability to adjust to developing innovations. Capability in computerized proficiency is fundamental for people exploring virtual work areas, online coordinated effort stages, and the mix of innovation into different businesses.

Remote work, advanced by worldwide occasions, has turned into a critical part of contemporary vocations. The capacity to work actually in virtual conditions, convey nonconcurrently, and influence computerized cooperation devices is fundamental for experts in different fields. Remote work offers adaptability yet in addition requires a restrained way to deal with using time productively, self-inspiration, and keeping up with balance between serious and fun activities.

Variety and incorporation are vital parts of reasonable and versatile vocations. Associations that focus on variety establish conditions that cultivate development, innovativeness, and a rich embroidery of viewpoints. People who effectively add to comprehensive work societies support their partners as well as position themselves as significant resources in different and dynamic groups.

Offsetting individual desires with cultural and ecological contemplations adds to the maintainability of vocations on a more extensive scale. The quest for significant work, lined up with one's qualities and cultural necessities, adds a layer of direction to vocations. Manageable vocations include adding to positive social effect, supporting moral practices, and taking into account the natural ramifications of expert decisions.

All in all, building economical and versatile professions is a complex undertaking that requires a proactive and all encompassing methodology. Ceaseless learning, versatility, strength, computerized education, and a guarantee to individual and expert development structure the groundwork of professions that endure everyday hardship and change. People who embrace the powerful idea of work, effectively deal with their vocations, and add to positive cultural and ecological results position themselves for outcome in the developing scene of vocations and callings.

7.3 Prospects for Future Jobs in Automated Industries

The scene of business is going through an extraordinary shift as mechanization and man-made consciousness (computer based intelligence) innovations become progressively coordinated into different ventures. This development brings the two difficulties and valuable open doors, reshaping the idea of work and provoking an interest for new ranges of abilities. Investigating the possibilities for future positions in robotized ventures requires a nuanced comprehension of the manners in which robotization is affecting various areas and the abilities that will be fundamental for the labor force of tomorrow.

One of the essential areas seeing massive changes because of robotization is producing. Computerized creation lines, mechanical frameworks, and high level apparatus are changing how products are delivered. While this mechanization prompts expanded effectiveness and decreased costs, it additionally adjusts the work scene inside the area. Occupations that include normal, redundant errands are bound to be mechanized, prompting a change in the expertise necessities for human laborers.

In the assembling business, the interest for abilities in mechanical technology programming, support of robotized frameworks, and information examination is on the ascent. Experts who can work together with machines, investigate specialized issues, and decipher information produced via robotized cycles will assume a pivotal part in guaranteeing the consistent mix of robotization in assembling. Additionally, as ventures embrace shrewd assembling rehearses, abilities connected with the Web of Things (IoT) and information examination become progressively significant.

The help business is likewise encountering a change in outlook driven via robotization. From client support chatbots to robotized clerk frameworks, organizations are consolidating man-made intelligence driven innovations to upgrade proficiency and further develop the client experience. While robotization smoothes out specific errands, it likewise sets out open doors for occupations that require a human touch, like jobs in client relationship the executives, administration customization, and client experience plan.

In medical services, mechanization is changing different parts of the business, from diagnostics to patient consideration. Simulated intelligence calculations are being utilized to dissect clinical information, decipher analytic pictures, and even aid drug disclosure. While mechanization in medical care further develops precision and effectiveness, it additionally brings about new jobs. Medical care experts who can use innovation, decipher simulated intelligence produced experiences, and guarantee the moral utilization of computerized frameworks are turning out to be progressively important.

The field of transportation is near the precarious edge of a significant change with the improvement of independent vehicles. Robotized frameworks in coordinated operations and conveyance are turning out to be more common, requiring talented experts who can configuration, keep up with, and regulate these advancements. Occupations connected with the advancement of independent frameworks, including computer programmers, information researchers, and mechanical technology trained professionals, are supposed to be sought after as the transportation business embraces robotization.

In the monetary area, robotization is changing the scene of undertakings connected with information examination, risk evaluation, and extortion recognition. Mechanical interaction computerization (RPA) is being used for routine and rule-based monetary tasks. This shift sets out open doors for monetary experts to zero in on essential navigation, monetary preparation, and client relationship the executives, accentuating the significance of abilities in information examination, AI, and vital reasoning.

The rural business is likewise going through a computerized change with the coordination of mechanization and accuracy cultivating innovations. Mechanized hardware, robots, and artificial intelligence driven frameworks are being utilized to advance harvest yields, screen soil wellbeing, and smooth out cultivating activities. This shift requires a labor force with skill in rural innovation, information science, and machine activity, flagging a takeoff from conventional cultivating jobs.

The energy area is utilizing robotization to enhance the age, dissemination, and utilization of energy. Brilliant matrices, mechanized observing frameworks, and man-made intelligence driven energy the executives are becoming vital pieces of the business. Occupations in energy mechanization require a mix of specialized abilities in information examination, programming, and frameworks the executives, as well as a comprehension of economical practices in energy creation.

The rise of savvy urban areas, portrayed by interconnected frameworks and computerized foundation, is setting out work open doors in metropolitan preparation, information examination, and IoT the board. Experts with mastery in metropolitan advances, maintainability, and information driven dynamic will be fundamental in forming the urban communities representing

things to come. The combination of mechanization in city the executives carries with it the potential for further developed effectiveness in transportation, energy utilization, and public administrations.

While the joining of mechanization into different ventures presents energizing prospects, it additionally raises worries about work uprooting and the requirement for upskilling and reskilling. Occupations that include normal, redundant errands are at a higher gamble of robotization, requiring a change in the labor force toward jobs that require extraordinarily human abilities. Delicate abilities like imagination, decisive reasoning, the capacity to appreciate people on a profound level, and versatility become progressively significant as standard undertakings become mechanized.

The idea of "half and half positions" is acquiring noticeable quality, featuring the requirement for people to have a mix of specialized abilities and human-driven abilities. Occupations that include complex critical thinking, inventiveness, and relational correspondence are less helpless to robotization. Half and half experts, who can explore both the specialized and human parts of their jobs, will be strategically set up in the gig market representing things to come.

In the domain of training, the interest for abilities connected with innovation and computerization is reshaping educational programs and instructing philosophies. The accentuation on STEM (science, innovation, designing, and math) training is driven by the acknowledgment that future positions will require a strong groundwork in these disciplines. Moreover, there is a developing accentuation on developing abilities like decisive reasoning, cooperation, and versatility to plan understudies for the powerful labor force.

State run administrations and associations are perceiving the significance of putting resources into labor force advancement projects to address the difficulties presented via mechanization. Upskilling drives, reskilling programs, and long lasting learning amazing open doors are being elevated to guarantee that the labor force stays lithe and furnished with the abilities requested via computerized businesses. Joint efforts between instructive organizations, organizations, and policymakers are fundamental to make a pipeline of ability prepared to flourish in the robotized future.

The moral ramifications of robotization likewise come to the front as machines take on dynamic jobs. Inquiries regarding algorithmic inclination, straightforwardness, and responsibility require cautious thought. Moral systems for the turn of events and utilization of simulated intelligence advances are essential to guarantee that robotization serves society's wellbeing and limits potentially negative side-effects.

7.4 The Continuous Evolution of Work in Automated Realities

The nonstop development of work in computerized real factors mirrors the powerful transaction between mechanical progressions, cultural changes, and the redefinition of customary business standards. As mechanization and man-made consciousness (artificial intelligence) advances become progressively incorporated into different enterprises, the idea of work goes through significant changes. Understanding this development requires an investigation of the complex variables molding the manner in which we work, the difficulties presented via mechanization, and the open doors it presents for a more deft and imaginative labor force.

One of the characterizing highlights of the mechanized the truth is the continuous shift from normal, monotonous undertakings to occupations that require interestingly human abilities. Mechanization succeeds at taking care of unsurprising and rule-based assignments, prompting the computerization of specific work capabilities. In any case, this likewise encourages an interest for abilities that are less helpless to mechanization, like imagination, decisive reasoning, the capacity to understand people on a deeper level, and complex critical thinking. The development of work in computerized real factors expects people to develop a different range of abilities that supplements the capacities of machines.

The gig economy, portrayed by present moment and independent commitment, is an unmistakable sign of the developing work scene. Empowered by computerized stages, the gig economy offers adaptability and independence for laborers while giving associations admittance to a different ability pool. The ascent of gig work difficulties customary ideas of business, bringing up issues about professional stability, benefits, and the social wellbeing net. As people explore the gig economy, the capacity to advertise oneself, deal with different activities, and adjust to changing workplaces becomes fundamental.

Remote work, advanced by worldwide occasions, is one more component of the developing work scene. Propels in correspondence advancements and cooperation devices have made it achievable for people to work from basically anyplace. The remote work model stresses adaptability, empowering representatives to accomplish a superior balance between serious and fun activities. Nonetheless, it likewise requires a reexamination of conventional administration rehearses, the foundation of clear correspondence channels, and the development of a virtual hierarchical culture. The mixture model, joining remote and in-person work, arises as a potential arrangement that obliges both adaptability and coordinated effort.

With regards to mechanized real factors, the connection among people and machines turns into a point of convergence. Cooperative robots, or cobots, work close by people in assembling, medical services, and different enterprises. Human-machine joint effort isn't restricted to actual undertakings; it reaches out to mental errands too. Increased insight, a cooperative connection among people and man-made intelligence, use machine capacities to improve human navigation.

The powerful combination of people and machines requires a cooperative outlook, computerized education, and a comprehension of the moral contemplations encompassing simulated intelligence.

Abilities improvement arises as a basic figure exploring the mechanized real factors of the labor force. Constant learning becomes basic as innovation develops, delivering specific abilities out of date and encouraging interest for new ones. Long lasting learning drives, both formal and casual, gain importance in engaging people to remain significant in the gig market. Associations assume a significant part in cultivating a culture of picking up, giving preparation programs, and working with open doors for expertise improvement.

The moral ramifications of robotization and man-made intelligence innovations come to the front as their impact penetrates different parts of work. Worries about algorithmic inclination, straightforwardness, and responsibility brief conversations about mindful man-made intelligence advancement and arrangement. The moral contemplations reach out to issues of information protection, security, and the potential for unseen side-effects. Building moral structures that guide the utilization of computerization innovations turns into an aggregate liability regarding legislatures, associations, and innovation designers.

Variety, value, and consideration (DEI) arise as key contemplations in the developing work scene. As businesses become more robotized, the significance of building different and comprehensive groups acquires conspicuousness. A different labor force brings changed points of view, encounters, and approaches, encouraging development and forestalling the propagation of predispositions in robotized frameworks. Associations that focus on DEI drives are better situated to draw in top ability and adjust to the changing socioeconomics of the worldwide labor force.

Administration in mechanized real factors takes on another aspect as associations explore the intricacies of a mechanically determined workplace. Pioneers should adjust the reconciliation of mechanization with the prosperity of their labor force, encouraging a culture of constant learning and flexibility. Dexterous administration, described by the capacity to answer change, advance development, and enable representatives, becomes instrumental in directing associations through the persistent development of work.

With regards to computerized real factors, the idea of "boundaryless vocations" gains pertinence. People are not generally bound to straight profession directions inside a solitary association. All things considered, they explore assorted vocation ways, embracing open doors for learning and development across various businesses and jobs. The capacity to turn, upskill, and move abilities between spaces turns into a sign of effective boundaryless professions.

The fate of work is unpredictably connected to the idea of direction driven associations. Representatives, especially the more youthful age, look for something other than a check; they look for arrangement with hierarchical qualities and a feeling of adding to a more noteworthy cultural reason. Reason driven associations focus on friendly and eco-logical obligation, drawing in people who are propelled by a feeling of significance and effect in their work.

The development of work in computerized real factors likewise in-volves a rethinking of hierarchical designs. Progressive models give way to additional spry, organized structures that work with cooperation, devel-opment, and versatility. Decentralized navigation, cross-useful groups, and an emphasis on results become key highlights of associations that flourish in computerized conditions. The accentuation on results over processes mirrors a shift toward execution based assessments.

The actual work area goes through change in light of the advancing idea of work. While remote work turns out to be more pervasive, the workplace isn't delivered old. All things considered, the workplace fills in as a center point for cooperation, imagination, and social communi-cation. Adaptable work areas, intended to oblige a mix of remote and in-person work, become fundamental. The actual climate is organized to encourage a feeling of local area, support prosperity, and upgrade efficiency.

The possibilities for future positions in mechanized real factors stretch out to arising fields and businesses. Online protection, information science, man-made consciousness, and sustainable power are among the areas encountering development as computerization turns out to be progressively incorporated into everyday activities. Occupations in these fields require particular abilities, making them appealing choices for people looking to adjust their vocations to the requests of the computerized future.

The schooling system turns into a pivotal player in setting up the labor force for the difficulties and chances of computerized real factors. Educational programs develop to consolidate computerized proficiency, decisive reasoning, and interdisciplinary methodologies. Instructive foundations team up with ventures to give active encounters, temporary jobs, and openness to arising advances. The objective is to furnish understudies with the abilities and outlook expected for a future where flexibility and persistent learning are principal.

Globalization stays a critical power forming the eventual fate of work in computerized real factors. The interconnectedness of economies, worked with by computerized advancements, sets out open doors for coordinated effort, ability versatility, and culturally diverse trade. Associations with a worldwide mentality are better situated to use different ability pools and explore the intricacies of working in an interconnected world.

The medical services industry, specifically, encounters remarkable changes as mechanization and man-made intelligence advancements are incorporated into clinical practices. Telemedicine, simulated intelligence helped diagnostics, and mechanical medical procedure are among the developments changing medical services conveyance. Occupations in wellbeing informatics, information examination, and medical services innovation the board become progressively applicable. The job of medical care experts develops to remember capability for advanced wellbeing innovations and the capacity to team up with robotized frameworks.

The crossing point of man-made consciousness and innovativeness turns into a critical part of work development. While computerization is skilled at taking care of routine undertakings, the inventive space stays a fortress of human creativity. Occupations in plan, content creation, and advancement gain conspicuousness as associations perceive the worth of human imagination in critical thinking and ideation. The capacity to think fundamentally, produce original thoughts, and take part in imaginative cooperation turns into a sought-after expertise in computerized real factors.

The moral contemplations encompassing the utilization of man-made intelligence and computerization advancements stretch out past predispositions in calculations. As independent frameworks pursue choices that influence people's lives, inquiries of straightforwardness, responsibility, and decency come to the very front. The moral turn of events and organization of man-made intelligence require interdisciplinary coordinated effort including technologists, ethicists, policymakers, and end-clients. Laying out moral systems and guidelines becomes basic to guarantee the dependable utilization of mechanization advances.

The job of the capacity to appreciate anyone on a profound level in store for work acquires noticeable quality as robotization turns out to be more common. Occupations that include sympathetic correspondence, relationship-building, and consistent encouragement are less inclined to be robotized. Human-driven jobs in guiding, medical care, and client assistance accentuate the significance of understanding and answering human feelings. The capacity to understand people on a profound level, combined with computerized proficiency, positions people to flourish in jobs that require a nuanced comprehension of human encounters.

The cultural effect of mechanization on business examples and pay circulation highlights the requirement for insightful approaches and social security nets. Widespread essential pay (UBI) turns into a subject of conversation as a likely answer for address the monetary incongruities coming about because of occupation dislodging. UBI proposes furnishing all residents with an ordinary, unrestricted amount of cash, guaranteeing a gauge way of life paying little heed to work status. The execution of such arrangements requires cautious thought of monetary ramifications, achievability, and cultural prosperity.

The idea of work-life coordination arises as a nuanced viewpoint on accomplishing balance in robotized real factors. Rather than a severe partition among work and individual life, people and associations investigate models that take into consideration adaptability and independence. Adaptable booking, remote work choices, and results-based assessments add to a workplace where people can coordinate their expert and individual obligations flawlessly. Accomplishing work-life joining turns into a common obligation among businesses and representatives.

The effect of mechanization on conventional training models prompts a reconsideration of the abilities and capabilities required for progress later on labor force. The accentuation on STEM (science, innovation, designing, and math) instruction is supplemented by a developing acknowledgment of the significance of STEAM (STEM + expressions) schooling. The mix of expressions and humanities close by specialized disciplines recognizes the worth of balanced schooling that encourages inventiveness, decisive reasoning, and interdisciplinary critical thinking.

The idea of long lasting learning develops into a foundation of profession improvement in robotized real factors. Persistent upskilling and reskilling become intrinsic to professional success as enterprises go through fast changes. Internet learning stages, miniature qualifications, and industry-explicit certificates gain fame as available roads for people to secure new abilities. The capacity to adjust and learn turns into a main trait of a versatile and deft labor force.

The mix of blockchain innovation, known for its decentralized and secure nature, impacts the scene of work in computerized real factors. Blockchain works with straightforward and sealed record-keeping, influencing enterprises, for example, finance, inventory network, and medical services. Occupations connected with blockchain improvement, brilliant agreement programming, and blockchain engineering arise as specific jobs requiring a profound comprehension of disseminated record innovations.

The cooperative idea of work is reclassified in mechanized real factors, with the ascent of cooperative robots (cobots) and virtual coordinated effort apparatuses. Human-machine joint effort turns into a foundation of effectiveness in assembling, coordinated factors, and, surprisingly, imaginative undertakings. Occupations in cooperative plan, human-robot communication, and virtual group the executives gain noticeable quality. The capacity to explore and use cooperative innovations turns into a fundamental expertise in a labor force that traverses physical and virtual spaces.

With regards to mechanized real factors, the roundabout economy gets forward momentum as an economical way to deal with asset the board. The round economy model intends to limit squander and expand the worth of assets by advancing reusing, reuse, and capable utilization.

Occupations connected with manageable practices, eco-plan, and waste decrease become basic in enterprises taking a stab at natural obligation. The round economy tends to environmental worries as well as sets out work open doors in green enterprises.

The job of neurodiversity in the working environment turns into a point of convergence as associations perceive the worth of different mental capacities. Neurodivergent people, for example, those with chemical imbalance, bring remarkable points of view and abilities that add to advancement and critical thinking. Associations that embrace neurodiversity establish comprehensive conditions, utilizing the qualities of people with assorted mental profiles. The acknowledgment of neurodiversity widens the comprehension of ability and likely in the labor force.

The extension of expanded reality (AR) and computer generated reality (VR) innovations acquaints new aspects with the workplace. AR and VR applications are utilized in preparing, distant coordinated effort, and recreation based learning. Occupations in AR and VR improvement, vivid experience plan, and 3D displaying become important in enterprises going from medical care to training. The capacity to explore virtual conditions and make vivid encounters turns into a significant range of abilities.

The medical services area encounters a change in outlook with the combination of telemedicine, wearable innovations, and artificial intelligence driven diagnostics. Far off quiet checking, virtual interviews, and customized medical care arrangements rethink the patient-specialist relationship. Occupations in wellbeing innovation, telehealth the executives, and information examination become basic for the successful execution of innovation in medical services. The crossing point of innovation and medical care sets out open doors for experts with skill in the two areas.

As ventures mechanize, the interest for talented online protection experts heightens. The rising network of gadgets and frameworks enhances the gamble of digital dangers and assaults. Occupations in online protection incorporate jobs like moral programmers, security experts, and network safety advisors. The capacity to safeguard delicate data, recognize weaknesses, and answer digital occurrences becomes fundamental in protecting mechanized frameworks.

The developing idea of work in mechanized real factors requires a reconsideration of conventional thoughts of administration. Versatile authority, portrayed by the capacity to explore change, encourage development, and engage groups, becomes vital. Pioneers in mechanized conditions should show a profound comprehension of innovation, moral direction, and the ability to motivate and direct groups through ceaseless changes. The accentuation shifts from various leveled control to cooperative and comprehensive initiative models.

The combination of mechanization in horticulture, known as accuracy cultivating, changes customary cultivating rehearses. Mechanized apparatus, sensor advances, and computer based intelligence driven examination streamline crop the board, asset use, and yield forecast. Occupations in accuracy horticulture include skill in information science, agritech, and advanced mechanics. The feasible and proficient acts of accuracy cultivating add to both expanded efficiency and diminished natural effect.

The moral contemplations encompassing the utilization of mechanization stretch out to the advancement of independent weapons and military innovations. Conversations about deadly independent frameworks brief discussions about the moral ramifications of assigning decision-production to machines in struggle circumstances. The moral turn of events and utilization of military mechanization advances require worldwide joint effort, straightforwardness, and adherence to moral principles to forestall potentially negative results and defend basic freedoms.

The ascent of advanced monetary forms and decentralized finance (DeFi) acquaints new aspects with the monetary business. Blockchain-based cryptographic forms of money, savvy contracts, and decentralized trades reshape customary monetary frameworks. Occupations in cryptographic money improvement, blockchain evaluating, and decentralized finance the executives become pertinent in a scene that embraces computerized monetary forms. The reconciliation of blockchain advancements in finance requires a nuanced comprehension of both monetary standards and conveyed record innovations.

In the domain of room investigation and satellite innovation, mechanization assumes a crucial part. Independent rocket, automated meanderers, and man-made intelligence driven information examination add to progressions in space investigation. Occupations in space innovation include jobs, for example, aviation design, satellite tasks, and space information examination. The investigation and usage of space deliver amazing open doors for joint effort between the general population and confidential areas, the scholarly community, and global space organizations.